Table of Contents

Section I. Introduction

"There is an aspect of military science which needs to be studied above all others in the Armed Forces: the capacity to adapt oneself to the utterly unpredictable, the entirely unknown."

— Sir Michael Howard[1]

The military defeat of Poland in 1939 was a miscalculated tragedy that led to Poland's demise as a sovereign nation. The cause of the tragedy spans back three centuries to the reign of King Stanislaw Augustus Poniatowski in 1764.[2] Since the eighteenth century, the Poles have pursued two primary strategic imperatives: independence from Russia and regional dominance in Eastern Europe. These strategic imperatives have historically led Poland to use its military as the primary way of achieving its imperatives.

This monograph analyzes how Poland used its military over recent centuries in order to provide a more complete understanding of why Poland fought without allies and met defeat in the opening days of the Second World War. Thus, the primary research question is how did Poland's enduring strategic imperatives shape its military and determine the use of its military in 1939? Answering this question informs readers how strategic imperatives may shape and determine the use of a nation's ways and means. Further, the question also serves to provide insight into how a military theory and doctrine evolves to satisfy political will.

Research Methodology

The model used to analyze the historical development and use of Poland's military to achieve Poland's strategic imperative is diplomacy, information, military, and economic (DIME). The model serves as the instrument for analyzing the linkage between the military and the strategic imperatives across four time-periods in Poland's history from 1764 to 1939. The specific time-periods are: (1) 1764-1918, The partitions of the Polish-Lithuanian Commonwealth to the

---

[1] Lacquement, Richard. "In the Army Now." The American Interest, http://www.the-american-interest.com/article.cfm?piece=860 (accessed September 12, 2011).

[2] W. Alison Phillips, *Poland* (New York: Henry Hold and Company), 66.

1

Second Polish Republic, (2) 1918-1926, The Treaty of Riga to Jozef Pilsudski's coup, (3) Pilsudski's coup to Pilsudski's death, (4) The rise of the Nazi war machine to Poland's military failure.

The analysis of each time-period begins with an introduction of the Polish strategic environment, vis-à-vis Europe, and then systematically highlights the diplomatic, information, military, and economic means available to Poland. Each time-period concludes that Poland never abandoned its strategic imperatives, despite limited resources and allies. The approach of introducing the strategic environment and highlighting means during each time-period provides a cohesive and logical structure in tracing the development and use of the Polish military across three centuries.

The last section, or conclusion, sums up the analysis from each time-period, provides additional points to ponder in understanding Poland's military defeat in 1939, and ultimately explains how strategic imperatives shape a military and affect its use. The DIME model also served as the criteria for selecting the literary sources used in writing this monograph.

The selected literature contained a broad array of primary, secondary, internet, journal, and scholarly sources. Drawing from such a broad pool of sources ensured a holistic understanding of how the military served to pursue Poland's strategic imperatives across three centuries. The literary sources were grouped into Polish diplomatic, information, military, and economic categories. Contained within each category are purely Polish historical sources and narratives that describe Poland's relationship with its European neighbors. The principal historical sources provided context for applying the DIME model.

The sources within the diplomatic category established the Polish strategic imperatives and described the Polish internal and external political environment between 1764 and 1939. Of the multitude of diplomatic sources, Norman Davies, Oscar Halecki, Richard Overy, Richard Watt, and Adam Zamoyski definitively articulated the Polish strategic imperatives and provided continuity of the pursuit of those imperatives.[3] Informational sources were linked closely with the diplomatic.

The literary material bounding the information category argued the internal and external Polish political situation throughout history and how the strategic imperatives resonated with the Polish people and their European neighbors. Specifically, works by Bohdan Budurowycz, Todd Fisher, Grace Humphrey, Lonnie Johnson, and Ferdynand Zweig gave a comprehensive overview of the arguments related to the Polish political situation and its relationship with diplomacy, the development and use of military force, and economics.[4]

With respect to military related publications, the literature ranged from broad concepts pertaining to military theory and doctrine, to the specific development and use of the Polish military. Of the publications considered, the writings of David Chandler, Carl von Clausewitz, Norman Davies, Azar Gat, Antoine-Henri Jomini, Peter Paret, Victor Madej, David Williamson, and Steven Zaloga presented critical insights on how Poland overwhelming used military means as the principle way of achieving its strategic imperatives. Further, the publications described how the Polish army initially aligned itself with the French military tradition, temporary abandoned with that tradition, and later resumed adhering to a French model in order to fight the combined German and Soviet armies in 1939.[5]

---

[3] Norman Davies, *God's Playground: A History of Poland, 1795 to the Present* (New York: Columbia University Press), 268; Oscar Halecki, *A History of Poland* (New York: Roy Publishers), 193; Richard Overy, *1939. Countdown to War* (New York: Viking), 10; Richard Watt, *Bitter Glory: Poland and its Fate, 1918-1939* (New York: Simon and Schuster), 97; Adam Zamoyski, *The Polish Way,* (New York: Hippocrene Books), 353.

[4] Bohdan Budurowycz, *Polish-Soviet Relations, 1932-1939* (New York: Columbia University Press), 3; and, Todd Fisher, *The Napoleonic Wars: The Empires Fight Back, 1808-1812* (London: Osprey Publishing), 29; and, Grace Humphrey, *Pilsudski: Builder of Poland* (New York, Scott and More), 162; and, Lonnie Johnson, *Central Europe: Enemies, Neighbors, and Friends* (Oxford: Oxford University Press), 128; and, Ferdynand Zweig, *Poland Between Two Wars* (London: Secker and Warburg), 47.

[5] David. G. Chandler, *The Campaigns of Napoleon* (New York: MacMillan Publishing Company), 528; and, Carl von Clausewitz, *On War* (Princeton: Princeton University Press), 198; and, Norman Davies, *White Eagle, Red Star* (London: Random House E-Books, 2003), under "Location 729 Amazon Kindle," Pimlico Electronic Book Edition; and, David Williamson, *Poland Betrayed. The Nazi-Soviet Invasions of 1939* (Mechanicsburg: Stackpole Books), 21; and, Steven Zaloga and Victor Madej, *The Polish Campaign 1939* (New York: Hippocrene Books, 1985), 15.

3

Norman Davies, Roman Debicki, Robert Machray, Samuel Sharp, Adam Zamoyski, and Ferdynand Zweig offered a broad historical account of the events between 1764 and 1939 and these sources aided in understanding the role of the Polish economy. Specifically, Robert Machray's writings lent detailed insight into the Polish economic state before and after the Great Depression and the impact the Depression had on Poland's military. What became clear was a military superior to Germany and the Soviet Union in the 1920s and later obsolete and inferior by the mid-1930s. The demise was highly attributed to the poor economic situation in Poland and its inability to shift from an agrarian to an industrial economy.[6]

Section II. 1764-1918: Partitions of the Polish-Lithuanian Commonwealth to the Second Polish Republic

The approximately one hundred and fifty years of Polish history from the partition of the Polish-Lithuanian Commonwealth to the end of the First World War illustrated some of the darkest days in the nation's history.[7] This section tells the story of how Poland established its two primary strategic imperatives of independence from Russia and achieving regional dominance. Moreover, it demonstrates Poland's inability to leverage diplomatic, information, and economic means in order to complement military force in achieving its strategic imperatives. As a consequence of the Polish passion for independence and regional dominance, the strategic imperative never waned and is pursued with military force, regardless if the means existed. Consequently, when Poland emerged as a new nation after the First World War, the Poles found themselves in border conflicts with Germany and at war with Russia.

---

[6] Robert Machray, *Poland 1914-1931* (London: George Allen and Unwin Ltd), 260; and, Samuel L. Sharp, *Poland. White Eagle on a Red Field* (Cambridge: Harvard University Press), 148; and, Adam Zamoyski, *The Polish Way* (New York: Hippocrene Books), 348; and, Ferdynand Zweig, *Poland Between Two Wars,* (London: Secker and Warburg), 47.

The Strategic Environment between 1764 and 1795: The Partitions of Polish-Lithuanian Commonwealth

In 1764, Stanislaw Augustus Poniatowski ascended to the Polish throne and became the Grand Duke of Lithuania amidst a violent power struggle. Using 20,000 troops from Catherine the Great's Army, and with political support from the Czartoryski family of Lithuania, Poniatowski quickly consolidated his claim (see Figure 1). Over time, Poniatowski grew tired of the persistent political interference from Russia in the Commonwealth's affairs. He envisioned a broader purpose for the Commonwealth that removed Russia's role as a protectorate and meddler in state affairs. In contrast, Catherine the Great, Empress of Russia, sought to expand her territory and maintain the balance of power in Europe by fighting the Ottoman Empire and forging a military alliance with Frederick the Great of Prussia.[8]

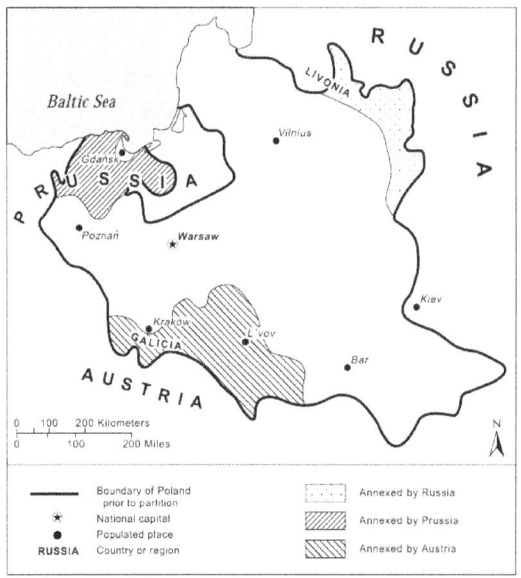

Figure 1: Before and after the First Partition of Poland, 1772.[9]

Despite existing between two powerful empires, Poniatowski planned to place the Commonwealth at the center of power within Eastern Europe. As a template for the future, he

---

[8] W. Alison Phillips, *Poland* (New York: Henry Hold and Company), 66-70; and, Adam Zamoyski, *The Polish Way, A Thousand Year History of the Poles and their Culture* (New York: Hippocrene Books), 225.
[9] U.S. Library of Congress, "The First Partition of Poland, 1772" http://memory.loc.gov/frd/cs/poland/pl01_03a.pdf (accessed January 5, 2012).

examined the Jagiellon dynasty of the sixteenth century, known as a period referred to as the Commonwealth's Golden Age, and found military dominance allowed the Jagiellon monarchs to amass territory and control one-third of the European mainland (see Figure 2).[10] Thus, Poniatowski believed a strong military was critical in achieving his imperatives.[11] While forging a fighting force capable of challenging Russia, Poniatowski used diplomacy to gain allies, projected a narrative of fighting for independence in the information realm, and worked to reform his agrarian economy. However, his primary way of achieving the Polish strategic imperative was by creating an Army of the Republic.

Figure 2: Polish-Lithuanian Commonwealth from the Union of Lublin, 1569 to 1667.[12]

---

[10] Adam Zamoyski, *The Polish Way, A Thousand Year History of the Poles and their Culture* (New York: Hippocrene Books), 50.

[11] Oscar Halecki, *A History of Poland* (New York: Roy Publishers), 193.

[12] U.S. Library of Congress, "The Polish-Lithuanian Commonwealth from the Union of Lublin, 1569 to 1667" http://lcweb2.loc.gov/cgi-bin/query/r?frd/cstdy:@field (DOCID+pl0019 (accessed March 5, 2012).

The use of DIME between 1764 and 1795: The Partitions of the Polish-Lithuanian Commonwealth

Poniatowski sought to use diplomacy in order to seek a change in the current political system that bound Poland to Russia. However, his diplomatic efforts created instability within the Commonwealth and across Europe because Poniatowski attempted to shift the balance of power in Europe in his favor.[13] To prevent a shift in the status quo, Catherine the Great and her allies fought Poniatowski and insurgents within Poland over a thirty-year period, which culminated in the series of three partitions in 1772, 1792, and 1795.[14] In all three instances, Poland fought without allies because the use of military force preceded Poland's ability to adequately build diplomatic support and leverage information and economic means.

Poniatowski's diplomatic strategy failed because Poland had no strategic incentive to offer other nations that would risk a change in the balance of power. Poland had an agrarian economy, little export capacity, a weak military, and a divided parliament mired in corruption and under the control of the Russian Empire. Further, with what little means were available to him, Poniatowski failed to appeal to Prussia and Austria, the only two powers within Central Europe capable of enabling Poland to achieve its strategic imperatives. When Prussia and Austria remained closed to the notion of Polish dominance, Poniatowski attempted to leverage the French. However, the likelihood of the French challenging Poland's enemies in the midst of their own internal social and economic reform was unrealistic. Further, the French contribution provided more akin to social and constitutional reform than military, and any military contribution would pale in comparison to the support lent during the American Revolution.[15] Hence, without a strategic incentive, Poniatowski's diplomatic appeals went unanswered.

In contrast, Russia and Prussia possessed mutually supporting incentives to maintain a long-standing partnership against Poland. Unknown to Poniatowski, Frederick and Catherine had

---

[13] Oscar Halecki, *A History of Poland* (New York: Roy Publishers), 193.
[14] Lonnie Johnson, *Central Europe: Enemies, Neighbors, and Friends* (Oxford: Oxford University Press), 128.
[15] Norman Davies, *Heart of Europe: A Short History of Poland* (Oxford: Oxford University Press), 251.

7

designs on ensuring a weakened Commonwealth existed between their two empires. In the pursuit of their strategic imperatives, Frederick desired consolidation of West and East Prussia and Catherine's attention focused on expelling the Turks from Russia.[16] Both monarchs agreed that Poland becoming a peer-competitor presented an obstacle on the path toward achieving their ambitions. Thus, Frederick and Catherine built a long-term military alliance against Poniatowski because both empires offered a mutually beneficial strategic incentive.

Poniatowski's diplomatic failure coincided within his shortcomings within the information realm. His inability to shape the discourse of his strategic message throughout Europe proved equally flawed within the Commonwealth's political body. Within Poland, the practice of forming political factions within a patronage system formed the basis for political power and Poniatowski threatened to change that framework. Moreover, nobles dominated the Parliament and maintained private armies to secure their private estates and economic holdings.[17] The mere thought of creating an Army of the Republic posed an unnecessary risk to the nobility's resources. Additionally, an army capable of challenging Russia would sever connections between the Commonwealth's nobility and Russian patrons.

Poniatowski engaged in an information campaign that sought sweeping constitutional reforms aimed at curtailing corruption and instituting social change that his opponents resisted. By the late 1760s, the Parliament became paralyzed and inundated with Russian bribes. Poniatowski persisted and engaged the nobility and the Polish people on a strategic message aimed at demonstrating that Russian influence and corruption were eroding the Commonwealth. In response to Poniatowski's narrative, Catherine the Great sought to assume greater control over the Commonwealth by conducting a counter-information campaign.[18]

Catherine appealed to the passions of social reformers and insisted on granting extended civil rights to confessions beyond just the Catholic Poles, such as Orthodox Christians and

---

[16] W. Alison Phillips, *Poland* (New York: Henry Hold and Company), 65.
[17] Norman Davies, *Heart of Europe: A Short History of Poland* (Oxford: Oxford University Press), 307.
[18] Oscar Halecki, *A History of Poland* (New York: Roy Publishers), 196-205.

8

Protestants. Additionally, she used her chief ambassador, Nicholas Repnin, to bribe nobles into adopting pro-Russian constitutional reforms within the Polish Parliament.[19] In short order, Catherine controlled the political discourse and influenced broader European opinion. With her information campaign in effect, she mobilized 40,000 troops on the Commonwealth's borders to demonstrate her resolve in extending her power and influence.[20]

With the threat of a Russian invasion from outside and internal strife inside the Commonwealth, Poniatowski lost political will and abandoned his strategic imperatives and allowed Catherine to reform the constitution. However, seams had already formed between the monarch and other nobles supporting the exclusiveness of Catholic civil liberties, anti-Russian sentiments, and a desire to undo Catherine's influence on the constitution.[21] Concerned over Poniatowski's kowtowing to Catherine's demands, the disenfranchised formed the Confederation of Radom, or Bar Confederation, in 1767.[22] The Confederation's aims were to depose Poniatowski, his supporters, such as the Czartoryski's of Lithuania, restore the constitution, and resume the Commonwealth's strategic imperatives.[23]

Amidst a rising rebellion, Poniatowski appealed to Russia in 1768 and supported the deployment of a Russian army into Polish lands in order to stop the rebellion.[24] In exchange for aid, Catherine demanded a Polish-Russian treaty to further subjugate the Commonwealth under Russian rule. Poniatowski had no choice but to agree. However, the Confederation resisted and fought a four-year conflict. By 1772, the combined forces of Prussia, Austria, and Russia drove the Confederation of Radom from Poland and completed the First Partition of the Commonwealth (See Figure 1). Later, as Poniatowski continued to abandon his strategic imperative, others resumed the cause. The most noteworthy was Thaddeus Kosciuszko's insurgency against

---

[19] W. Alison Phillips, *Poland* (New York: Henry Hold and Company), 65.
[20] James Fletcher, *The History of Poland,*175.
[21] Dionysius Lardner, *The History of Poland in One* Volume, (London: A&R Spottiawoode), 238.
[22] Ibid., 238-40.
[23] Oscar Halecki, *A History of Poland*, 194.
[24] W. Alison Phillips, *Poland* (New York: Henry Hold and Company), 64-69; Oscar Halecki, *A History of Poland*, 196.

Poniatowski during the Uprising of 1794. However, all attempts at pursuing the strategic imperative against Russia failed. In sum, the persistent use of military force without allies, guarantees for support from other nations, and an agrarian economy, further fractured Poland until it collapsed.[25]

While the Commonwealth faced multiple military defeats, the partition period gave rise to the formation of the Army of the Republic when Poniatowski first pursued his strategic imperatives. The Army of the Republic formed the basis for the resistance against Russia and her allies in the late eighteenth century and later laid the foundation for Napoleon's Polish Legions. To create the army, Poniatowski consolidated many of the private armies and militias back in 1765.[26] As mentioned, this action led to contention with the nobles that controlled many private armies.

While creating a national army, Poland championed the primacy of the cavalry and its ability to provide rapid mobility and maintain tempo across the flat and open terrain of Central and Eastern Europe. While infantry and artillery were considered important elements within the army, they were secondary to cavalry education and training at military academies.[27] However, some efforts to integrate infantry and artillery with the cavalry existed within the national military academy in Warsaw.[28] Over time, Warsaw became the centralized location for military training in Poland.

As the academies focused on developing cavalry tactics, there was an effort to defend the Commonwealth by constructing fortresses. Specifically, Jan Bakatowicz's defensive military theory and doctrine, borrowed from French theorist Sebastian le Prestre de Vauban, emphasized the construction or improvement a fortifications along key terrain within the realm. Consequently,

---

[25] Oscar Halecki, *A History of Poland*, 196, 254; W. Alison Phillips, *Poland* (New York: Henry Hold and Company), 64-69; Oscar Halecki, *A History of Poland*, 196.

[26] Norman Davies, *God's Playground: A History of Poland, 1795 to the Present* (New York: Columbia University Press), 268.

[27] Oscar Halecki, *A History of Poland* (New York: Roy Publishers), 193.

[28] Norman Davies, *God's Playground: A History of Poland, 1795 to the Present* (New York: Columbia University Press), 268.

the capital city of Warsaw, the Commonwealth's shared border with Russia, and major river systems received significant upgrades to their defensive posture.[29]

Using the doctrine and theory described, the military performed well, despite a lack of resources and clear operational and strategic aims. As mentioned, the Bar Confederation held against a superior force during four years of conflict by capitalizing on the education provided within the academies and using a portion of the national army in their insurgency efforts.[30] The military prowess displayed by Poles on both sides of the Bar Confederation conflict led to an increase in the size of the national army. By 1788, the Army of the Republic grew to 100,000 men.[31] Unfortunately, Poland's army proved inadequate to challenge the combined might of Russia, Prussia, and Austria. During the Second and Third Partitions of Poland, Russia amassed Polish territory and eventually dissolved Poland. Poniatowski abdicated his throne in 1795.[32]

During each partition of the Commonwealth, the economy steadily progressed into ruin. For centuries, the Polish-Lithuanian Commonwealth's economy existed as agrarian with few exports throughout Europe. With persistent political strife and conflict, Poniatowski never succeeded in converting to an industrial economy. After Poniatowski relinquished his pursuit of the strategic imperatives, and others resumed the cause, the economic means never materialized.

Specifically, the economic impact of the First Partition proved unrecoverable and laid the groundwork for the inevitable destruction of the Commonwealth's economy. Moreover, after 1772, the Commonwealth lost over a third of its territory and vital commercial and industrial

---

[29] Norman Davies, *God's Playground: A History of Poland, 1795 to the Present* (New York: Columbia University Press), 267-270.
[30] Lonnie Johnson, *Central Europe: Enemies, Neighbors, and Friends* (Oxford: Oxford University Press), 128.
[31] Norman Davies, *God's Playground: A History of Poland, 1795 to the Present* (New York: Columbia University Press), 269.
[32] James Fletcher, *The History of Poland from the Earliest Period to the Present Time* (New York: Harper and Brothers), 256.

11

centers.[33] In particular, the seizure of Northwest Poland denied over eighty percent of the

Commonwealth's trade and became a source of economic consternation well into the 1920s.[34]

Additionally, when Russia tore Lithuania from Poland in the 1770s, over one-third of the

Commonwealth's population, mostly non-Polish, became citizens of foreign powers. The

Lithuanians represented a wealthy nucleus of the Commonwealth and without Lithuania, Poland

relied on its agrarian economy to challenge Catherine's authority. The agrarian economy stood in

start contrast to the industrial revolution starting to sweep across Europe.

Without a strong economy, Poland's military remained obsolete and unable to achieve

Poland's strategic imperatives. By 1795, Poland was a shell of its former glory. The Third

Partition in that year effectively destroyed any remaining vestige of the Polish Kingdom and

formally subordinated the former monarchy under the dominion of the Russians, Prussians, and

Austrians (see Figure 3).[35] The last partition also removed Poland's ability to disrupt the balance

of power and allowed Russia and Prussia the opportunity to pursue their strategic imperatives

unabated until Napoleon Bonaparte.

Figure 3: Third Partition of Poland, 1795.[36]

[33] Oscar Halecki, *A History of Poland* (New York: Roy Publishers), 204.
[34] Ibid., 204-206.
[35] Ibid., 126-129.
[36] U.S. Library of Congress, "The Third Partition of Poland, 1795"
http://lcweb2.loc.gov/frd/cs/poland/pl01_03c.pdf (accessed January 5, 2012).

An examination of DIME between 1764 and 1795 revealed the establishment of the Polish strategic imperatives by King Poniatowski after assuming the Commonwealth's throne. In time, Poniatowski looked back to the Jagiellon dynasty for inspiration in achieving independence from Russia and achieving regional dominance in Eastern Europe. Hence, Poniatowski determined the primary way of achieving his vision was by building a national army capable of challenging Russia.

While building the new army, Poniatowski unsuccessfully engaged in diplomatic and information-based endeavors in order to secure allies across Europe and within the Parliament. In addition, he sought to convert from an agrarian to an industrial economy. However, his understanding of the strategic environment proved incomplete and Catherine the Great successfully outmaneuvered Poniatowski by leveraging all of Russia's national instruments of power. The net result was a destroyed Polish Kingdom, an instilled insurgency spirit within the Polish consciousness, and a desire to resume the strategic imperatives by finding a strong ally. The arrival of Napoleon Bonaparte presented another opportunity.

The Strategic Environment between 1807-1815: Duchy of Warsaw

Geographically, the Duchy of Warsaw constituted the Prussian holdings from the Second and Third Partitions with a population of nearly two million Poles (see Figure 4). The Duchy was established in 1807 after Napoleon defeated the Prussians and initially served as a base of operations to support Napoleon's Grande Armée. Moreover, Napoleon capitalized on Poland's desire to resume their strategic imperative of independence and regional dominance. Hence, he found at least 50,000 trained soldiers willing to enlist to his cause. The Poles fighting for Napoleon had the mistaken belief that since France recently underwent a social revolution, the French would support the Polish cause for independence. This fundamental mismatch in the basic understanding of why they were fighting and Napoleon's true designs on Poland caused the Poles to face swift retribution by Russia after Napoleon's defeat in 1815.[37]

Figure 4: Duchy of Warsaw, 1807-13, and Congress Poland, 1815.[38]

The use of DIME between 1807-1815: Duchy of Warsaw

Napoleon understood the importance of not unduly upsetting the balance of power in Central and Eastern Europe better than Poniatowski and the insurgent successors of the Polish strategic imperatives. Since he understood the power and influence relationships within Europe, Napoleon never had any intentions of restoring the Polish-Lithuanian Commonwealth. While dealing with Poland, Napoleon acted with caution. The emperor knew that empowering the Poles too much risked a Polish insurgency against Russia, Prussia, and Austria. More to the point, France would find itself fighting on multiple fronts with Poland at the center of conflict. Hence, the Polish revolutionary and militaristic spirit required tempering.

Within Prussia and Austria diplomatic circles, Napoleon maintained that the Duchy of Warsaw was a French vassal state with a large preponderance of the French Army on Polish

[37] David. G. Chandler, *The Campaigns of Napoleon* (New York: MacMillan Publishing Company), 514,1092; and, Oscar Halecki, *A History of Poland* (New York: Roy Publishers), 739.
[38] U.S. Library of Congress, "Duchy of Warsaw, 1807-13, and Congress Poland, 1815" http://lcweb2.loc.gov/frd/cs/poland/pl01_04a.pdf (accessed January 5, 2012).

soil.[39] By creating a Duchy, Napoleon achieved temporary stability and peace with Prussia and Austria. Without the threat of war from Prussia and Austria, the Duchy existed to secure Napoleon's flank in his march towards Russia and provided a secure lines of communication back to France.[40]

With respect to Napoleon's informational approach, he capitalized on the opportunity to appeal to the Polish desire for independence by instilling the Napoleonic Code. The Code served to reform the Polish social, economic, and military structure. Through army reform, Napoleon successfully instilled pride within the Polish people and gave them the false hope of achieving independence. Moreover, by installing his own vassal as the Grand Duke of Poland, Napoleon kept abreast of the internal dialogue within the Duchy's Parliament and shaped a political discourse that advocated for his conquest of Russia.

From the perspective of the military, Napoleon's theory and doctrine had a profound influence in creating the Polish Legions. For the Poles, the Polish Legions represented the only practical means and way of gaining independence and becoming a regional power. Under the Napoleonic Code, which outdated old feudal laws of governance based on nobility and birth entitlements, the Duchy invested in the education of its soldiers and promoted its ranks based on merit.[41] Further, citizens of the Duchy served France based on six-year conscription and introduced the notion of the citizen soldier.[42] The establishment of a three-year officer and senior non-commissioned officer National Application Course built around the new officer cadre signified the formation and re-commitment of the Poles to a professional standing army.[43]

By 1809, The Duchy of Warsaw's Army swelled to 50,000 and was organized into the Vistula Legion and three divisions representing a mixed force of infantry, cavalry and artillery. In

---

[39] Todd Fisher, *The Napoleonic Wars: The Empires Fight Back, 1808-1812* (London: Osprey Publishing), 29.
[40] Archibald Alison, *History of Europe from the Fall of Napoleon in 1815 to the Accession of Louis Napoleon in 1852* (London: William Blackwood and Sons), 115.
[41] Norman Davies, *Heart of Europe: A Short History of Poland* (Oxford: Oxford University Press), 163.
[42] Ibid., 268-270.
[43] Ibid., 266-272.

total, there were twenty-one infantry regiments, sixteen cavalry regiments attached to the infantry, and three battalions of foot artillery and sappers. Napoleon was keen to deploy the Polish army away from Polish soil and it fought with distinction. During the Battle of Somosierra in Spain, Napoleon hailed the Polish Lancers as the bravest cavalrymen in his army and integrated them into his elite Old Guard. With each military success, came the will to invest in increasing the capabilities of the Duchy's Army. By 1812, the Army doubled in size to 100,000 men and prepared to liberate Lithuania and support the invasion of Russia.[44]

Under the Duchy of Warsaw, the economy remained largely agricultural and revenues served to support Napoleon's Army. Moreover, the British succeeded in curtailing France's economy through blockades and manipulation of the Continental System. Consequently, the Duchy's economic surplus flowed into France to offset financial shortfalls and war debts, leaving little for investing in the Duchy's infrastructure.[45] In sum, almost no significant economic changes occurred between Poniatowski's reign and Napoleon's Duchy of Warsaw. After Napoleon's defeat in 1815, the Poles struggled to rebuild an economy that served to support the military might of France for over a decade.

A consideration of DIME during the Duchy of Warsaw period reveals a continuation of the Polish strategic imperatives by supporting Napoleon's conquest of Europe. Napoleon skillfully capitalized on the Polish insurgent and militaristic spirit to enlist thousands into his Grande Armée. Moreover, he leveraged all instruments of national power to seek his own strategic imperatives. In particular, Napoleon proved adept at influencing the diplomatic and information realms.

Napoleon placated the Polish spirit of independence, pacified Prussia and Austria by not restoring the Polish Kingdom, and shaped the political discourse within the Duchy's parliament to

---

[44] Najder, Jacek. "Polish Cavalrymen in the French Imperial Guard." Permanent Delegation of the Republic of Poland to North Atlantic Treaty Organization. http://www.brukselanato.polemb.net/index.php? (accessed January 12, 2012); and, Robert Bruce, Iain Dickie, Keven Kiley, et al, *Fighting Techniques of the Napoleonic Age: 1872-1815, Equipment, Combat Skills, and Tactics* (New York: St. Martin's Press), 97.
[45] David. G. Chandler, *The Campaigns of Napoleon* (New York: MacMillan Publishing Company), 1009.

support war against Russia. Napoleon also maneuvered effectively in military and economic matters. Militarily, Napoleon's Army proved the finest in Europe and the influence of French theory and doctrine formed the basis for an enduring Franco-Polish military alliance that persisted into the twentieth century. Economically, the Duchy served to mitigate France's war debts and little change occurred toward an industrial economy.

When the Congress at Vienna met in 1815, after Napoleon's defeat, the Duchy of Warsaw dissolved and much of its territory reformed as the Congress Kingdom.[46] The Congress Kingdom existed as a Russian protectorate. During the Congress Kingdom period, and throughout the remainder of the eighteenth century, the desire to achieve the Polish strategic imperatives using military force never waned. Most notably, during the Congress Kingdom period, the November Uprising of 1830 to 1831 represented an ill-advised and near spontaneous insurgency against the Russian Empire by Polish military officers and cadets in Warsaw.[47]

Many within the Congress Kingdom and throughout Europe opposed the violent uprising, since by most accounts, the Congress Kingdom represented a deliberate Russian attempt at extended self-governance to Poland. Thus, acting with military action without first building international appeal and internal consensus resulted in condemnation from the Catholic Church and swift military defeat.[48] In this case, it appeared as though the hubris of fighting at any cost for independence and relying on the false hope that others would appeal on the Polish behalf appealed too strongly to the passions of the Polish people.

The Strategic Environment between 1914-1918: The First World War

During the First World War, Poland as a nation did not formally participate, but Poles fought for both sides during the conflict. Still, as in decades past, the pursuit of the Polish

---

[46] David. G. Chandler, *The Campaigns of Napoleon* (New York: MacMillan Publishing Company), 1009.
[47] Oscar Halecki, *A History of Poland* (New York: Roy Publishers), 232.
[48] Pope Gregory XVI, "Encyclical of Pope Gregory XVI on Civil Obedience on 9 June 1832." Eternal World Television Network Website. http://www.ewtn.com/library/ENCYC/G16CUMPR.HTM (accessed January 13, 2012).

17

strategic imperatives endured and independence from Russian control remained the primary aim. Thus, exiled Poles petitioned the French and the United States for supporting the Polish independence movement and the establishment of a new Polish state after the war. Further, it was the hope that after Poland became a nation, its allies would provide security and economic support. At the conclusion of the First World War, Poland did regain its independence, but faced a host of challenges, ranging from building diplomatic support for its expansion in Eastern Europe, garnering international appeal to stem the rise of communism, and rebuilding its armed forces and economy.

The use of DIME between 1914-1918: The First World War

The Polish use of DIME during the First World War primarily focused on two areas: gaining French and American appeal for the creation of a Polish State and creating a Polish Army capable of winning the war against the Central Powers. As in previous time-periods, the Poles believed their military contribution and prowess on the battlefield would translate into international appeal in supporting the Polish strategic imperatives. During the war, the Poles fought valiantly. By war's end, President Woodrow Wilson specifically advocated for the restoration of Poland during his Fourteen Points address to the Allied Powers and the Polish military in France served valiantly.[49]

In total, over two million Poles served within the armies of the Central Powers and the Triple Entente. As stated, the military functioned as the primary way of securing independence.[50] Moreover, embedded within the military were political factions vying for French and American diplomatic support, prestige in order to shape Polish politics after the war, and control of the future of the national army and economy. With respect to the principle military problem immediately after the war, the primary challenged rested with how to codify the disparate military

---

[49] Roman Debicki, *Foreign Policy of Poland, 1919-1939* (New York: Praeger), 6.
[50] Michael Krupinsky, "The Polish Army in France, World War I." Haller's Army. http://www.hallersarmy.com/ (accessed January 12, 2012).

theory and doctrine from many different nations into a cohesive doctrine. Further, who to designate to lead the army proved equally daunting. During the war, two competing theories and doctrines emerged with coinciding champions that fought for political and military control.

The Blue Army in France, or Polish Legion, formed in 1917 and most of the army's ranks were filled with volunteers from former Polish immigrants to America and displaced persons from the war. Under the command of Jozef Haller, and sponsored by the Polish politician Roman Dmowski, the army trained in the French tradition and favored the primacy of the infantry, defensive firepower via artillery, and trench warfare. The training and experiences the Blue Army gained from fighting with the French, and Dmowski's political influence, renewed the Franco-Polish military partnership from the Duchy of Warsaw and formed the basis for a continuous French military assistance mission to Poland lasting until the late 1930s. At the end of hostilities, the Blue Army consisted of about 50,000 men.[51]

In contrast to the Blue Army, Jozef Pilsudski's Polish Legions fought for the Germans and Austrians against Russia. Like Haller and Dmowski, Pilsudski's efforts were politically motivated and aimed at achieving the Polish strategic imperatives of deposing Russia's hold over Poland and positioning Poland in a place of power at the end of the war.[52] As a member of the Polish Socialist Party, Pilsudski garnered support by advocating for an independent Poland, universal voting rights, freedom of the press, and equal rights for all citizens. Pilsudski's Polish Legions, a force of about 40,000, trained and fought with cavalry as the primary fighting unit, embraced a highly maneuverable style of warfare, and placed the emphasis on individuals planning and executing battles versus a general officers staff advocated by the French.[53]

---

[51] Michael Krupinsky, "The Polish Army in France, World War I." Haller's Army. http://www.hallersarmy.com/ (accessed January 12, 2012); and, Maciej Jonascz, "The Poles in World War I." *Strategy and Tactics*, January 2012; and, Richard Watt, *Bitter Glory: Poland and its Fate, 1918-1939* (New York: Simon and Schuster), 113.

[52] Grace Humphrey, *Pilsudski: Builder of Poland* (New York, Scott and More), 162.

[53] Richard Watt, *Bitter Glory: Poland and its Fate, 1918-1939* (New York: Simon and Schuster), 113.

At the end of the war, Pilsudski and Dmowski competed for power, but Pilsudski emerged as a national hero and later became Head of State and Marshal of the Army after Poland was restored. Consequently, Pilsudski's Polish Legions formed the core of Poland's new national army, but faced significant challenges with integrating Haller's Blue Army. For political reasons that provided Poland security against Russia and Germany, Pilsudski welcomed French military and economic assistance. However, he preferred to develop the Polish military independently.[54]

A short examination of DIME from a Polish perspective during the First World War indicated again the important role the military played in achieving the Polish strategic imperatives. The conflict between Dmowski and Pilsudski demonstrated how interrelated were the military ways within the diplomatic and information means used in restoring Poland. After the war, Pilsudski led the new Polish nation, largely because of his appeal as a war hero and status as the defender of Polish independence against Russia. Still, as Dmowski and Pilsudski vied for political and military power, the Poles lost valuable time in sending a unified message to allies on where the new nation stood in terms of pursuing its enduring strategic imperatives. This became problematic after Pilsudski decided to resume the Polish strategic imperative created by Poniatowski in the eighteenth century.

Section III. 1918-1926: Polish-Russian War to Pilsudski's Coup

The initial eight years after the end of the First World War was characterized as a period of restoring Polish prestige and securing its place as the dominant power in Eastern Europe. Like his predecessors, Pilsudski's approach toward achieving the Polish strategic imperatives rested on a disproportionate use of military means. While independent from Russia, Pilsudski viewed Russia as the principle threat toward Polish sovereignty and sought to secure Poland's borders with military force. Pilsudski's approach dangerously paralleled Poniatowski's, but with one clear

---

[54] Grace Humphrey, *Pilsudski, Builder of Poland*, 166; and, Richard Watt, *Bitter Glory: Poland and its Fate, 1918-1939* (New York: Simon and Schuster), 60,110-113.

exception. Pilsudski never waved from the strategic imperatives and sent a consistent narrative to

his allies and enemies that Poland maintained an unrelenting desire to become a regional power.

Only after Pilsudski surrendered political authority to a successor did Poland begin a path toward

rapid social and economic decline. This decline prompted Pilsudski to stage a coup.

The Strategic Environment between 1918-1926: Polish-Russian War to Pilsudski's Coup: 1918-1926

The defeat of the Central Powers and the toppling of the Tsarist monarchy during the

First World War broke Poland free from Russian domination. However, as a Pole gazed in any

direction, he found himself surrounded by enemies. To complicate matters, the Treaty of

Versailles and the Paris Peace Conference left many unanswered questions concerning the

legitimacy of Poland's territory.[55] As the months passed with no diplomatic resolution, Pilsudski

made preparations to secure by force what was increasingly unattainable by diplomacy. The

immediate strategic imperative was simple, yet daunting. Pilsudski planned to restore the 1772

borders of the former Polish Kingdom and gain allies with Poland as the nucleus of Eastern

European affairs.[56] To achieve such an imperative required leveraging diplomacy, informational,

and economic influence. Central to the pursuit was the creation of a new national army.

The use of DIME between 1918-1926: Polish-Russian War to Pilsudski's Coup: 1918-1926

Any notions of conducting long-term peaceful diplomatic negotiations for the final

establishment of Poland's borders and the forming of long-term Eastern European allies

evaporated in the opening months of 1919. Less than a year after becoming a new nation, Poland

fought the Ukraine, acquired some of their territory, and disputed with the Germans over

---

[55] Yale Law School, "The Versailles Treaty, June 28, 1919," (Yale Law School Website, 2011), http://avalon.law.yale.edu/imt/partiii.asp (accessed November 13, 2011).

[56] Roman Debicki, *Foreign Policy of Poland, 1919-1939* (New York: Praeger), 18.

plebiscites along the German-Polish border.[57] In an attempt to shape the international and internal political discourse, Pilsudski sought to justify military action for expanding into Eastern Europe and along the German border by attempting to tap into the collective fear of a resurgent German and Russian military state. However, Poland's militaristic nature only antagonized its neighbors.

Pilsudski's message of Poles fighting to secure its borders failed to appeal to Western Europeans. This is especially true because after the First World War, 500,000 Germans, part of the German Oberkommando-Ostfront, still remained between Poland and Russia along a 1,500 mile front separating the two nations.[58] The force existed to contain Russian westward expansion, and to a lesser degree, deter Poland's aggressive nature. The latter point seemed valid, considering Poles had quickly conducted military action in the Ukraine.[59] Further, once the Germans vacated the region in February 1919, the Poles and Russians wasted no time filling the void to acquire territory. Lithuania fell first to the Russians. Pilsudski seized the opportunity to expand Polish territory and fight the Russians by proclaiming the latter as compelling Poland into war by attacking an ancestral ally.[60]

In what later evolved into the Polish-Russian War, The Poles and Russians engaged in a conflict Winston Churchill described as a struggle to prevent the spread of communism.[61] While brief, the war is significant since the campaign achieved most of Pilsudski's strategic imperatives, but fell short of placing Poland as the dominant power in Eastern Europe. However, the war demonstrated Poland's military potential to win against the Russians and offer security to potential Western European allies. After the war, Poland briefly served as an effective buffer against Russian expansion in Eastern Europe, and other nations began to see the strategic value in investing in Poland's economy and helping to rebuild its military. The other effect the war had

---

[57] Roman Debicki, *Foreign Policy of Poland, 1919-1939* (New York: Praeger), 16-21.
[58] Richard Watt, *Bitter Glory: Poland and its Fate, 1918-1939* (New York: Simon and Schuster), 94.
[59] Ibid., 94-97.
[60] Oscar Halecki, *A History of Poland* (New York: Roy Publishers), 286.
[61] Bohdan Budurowycz, *Polish-Soviet Relations, 1932-1939* (New York: Columbia University Press), 3.

was that it provided the Polish military the chance to develop a theory and doctrine that best suited their style of warfighting and capabilities.

Jominian theory and doctrine initially guided the Polish war planning efforts, but elements of Clausewitz are apparent, such as seeking decisive battle, versus using established lines of communication and methodically building combat power. In planning to seize the Lithuanian capital of Vilna from the Russians, the Poles believed the key to victory rested with delivering a decisive blow and interdicting lines of communication providing support from Moscow. Further, the Polish Military's High Command believed a significant victory would give the Russians second thoughts about escalating the war. Since the terrain was flat and open, the Poles relied on cavalry to regain the initiative. Also, because the Poles had portions of their army allocated along the Ukrainian, Czechoslovakian, and German borders, the initial force consisted of about 10,000 organized as a Northern and Southern Group. The main effort consisted of a minimum of twelve cavalry squadrons, twelve battalions of infantry and three artillery companies.[62]

In order to seize Vilna, Pilsudski incorporated surprise and deception into his tactics. Surprise and deception are highlighted within Jomini's *Art of War* as effective tactics for cavalry, but the effects the Poles achieved with these tactics are more akin to Clausewitz.[63] In *On War*, Clausewitz stated that surprise becomes the means to gain superiority, and when combined with speed at the decisive point, can psychologically defeat the enemy.[64]

Using surprise and deception, Pilsudski focused the brunt of his attack toward the city of Lina in the southeast, and drew a sizable portion of the opposition out of Vilna. With Vilna depleted and the Russians fixed at Lina with infantry and artillery, the cavalry interdicted the rail

---

[62] Richard M. Watt, *Bitter Glory, Poland and its Fate 1918 to 1939* (New York: Simon and Schuster), 97-100; and, Elbert Farman, "The Polish-Bolshevik Cavalry Campaigns of 1920," *The Cavalry Journal* 30, no. 122 (January 1921): 223; and, Norman Davies, *White Eagle, Red Star* (London: Random House E-Books, 2003), under "Location 729-735 Amazon Kindle," Pimlico Electronic Book Edition.
[63] Antoine Henri De Jomini, *The Art of War* (London: Greenhill Books), 209.
[64] Carl von Clausewitz, *On War* (Princeton: Princeton University Press), 198.

lines and isolated the Russians at both locations. With the opposition isolated, Vilna fell in three days. Capitalizing on the success at Vilna, the Pilsudski pushed further east and attacked Minsk. Similar to Vilna, the Poles first cut of vital logistics with cavalry by conducting raids around the city before attacking it directly. By understanding the importance of mobility, lines of communication, deception and surprise, Pilsudski's forces secured Lithuania and Belorussia by August of 1919.[65]

Both armies paused for the remainder of the year and the war reached its peak when action resumed in 1920. While resting, the both sides continued to build up their forces and organized them into separate army groups that could attack anywhere from Lithuania in the north and from the Ukraine in the south. The Polish High Command defined the area of operations as the land between the Vistula River and the Dnieper River (see Figure 5). Key terrain included the Pripet Marshes and two mobility corridors. The first was the White Ruthenian Gate, a three hundred mile northern passage that connected Minsk to Warsaw.[66] Contesting this space was the Russian's main effort commanded by Mikhail Tukhachevsky. Tukhachevsky's Army of the West consisted of the Fourth, Fifteenth, Third, and Sixteenth Armies.[67] The second corridor was the Volhynian Gate in the South, a two hundred mile approach following the Dniester and Pripet rivers, cutting across Belorussia and the Ukraine.[68] Rail and road to and from Kiev provided logistical support to the entire southern region. Providing opposition in the South was Alexander Yegorov's Army of the Southwest, consisting of the Twelfth and Fourteenth Armies.[69]

---

[65] Richard M. Watt, *Bitter Glory, Poland and its Fate 1918 to 1939* (New York: Simon and Schuster), 98; Adam Zamoyski, *Warsaw 1920* (London: Harper Collins), 9; and, Norman Davies, *White Eagle, Red Star* (London: Random House E-Books, 2003), under "Location 1052 Amazon Kindle," Pimlico Electronic Book Edition.

[66] Oscar Halecki, "Imperialism in Slavic and East European History", The American Association for the Advancement of Slavic studies, *American Slavic and East European Review,* Vol 11, No. 1 (February 1952), http://www.jstor.org/stable/2491662 (accessed November 14, 2011).

[67] Richard M. Watt, *Bitter Glory, Poland and its Fate 1918 to 1939* (New York: Simon and Schuster), 116.

[68] Dave Obee, "Volhynia", (Website on Volhynia history, 2011), http://www.volhynia.com/history.html, (accessed November 12, 2011).

[69] Richard M. Watt, *Bitter Glory, Poland and its Fate 1918 to 1939* (New York: Simon and Schuster), 118.

24

The Poles assessed that the defeat of Tukhachevsky's Army would signal the defeat of the Russian forces and put pressure on Moscow to end the war. What is interesting is that rather than choose a Jominian direct approach of concentrating the bulk of Polish forces in order to decisively defeat Tukhachevsky, Pilsudski chose an indirect approach by attacking Yegorov in the south. His rationale for doing so was both political and military. By attacking in the Ukraine, Pilsudski sought to liberate the nation and gain a long-term ally and immediate military support in the fight against the Russians.[71]

Pilsudski's decision to use an indirect approach fits neatly with Clausewitz's discussion of the destruction of enemy forces. In seeking to destroy enemy forces, Clausewitz pointed out that one might choose a direct or indirect approach.[72] Regardless of the chosen approach, it must contribute toward the satisfaction of the strategic or political aim.[73] In Pilsudski's case, the

---

[70] Harold Worrell, Jr., "Battle of Warsaw, 1920: Impact on Operational Thought" http://www.dtic.mil/cgi-bin/GetTRDoc?AD=ADA284723&Location=U2&doc=GetTRDoc.pdf (accessed January 5, 2012).
[71] Viscount D'Abernon, *The Eighteenth Decisive Battle of the World* (London: Hodder and Stoughton), 26.
[72] Carl von Clausewitz, *On War* (Princeton: Princeton University Press), 529.
[73] Ibid., 529-531.

indirect approach of seizing the Ukraine for political and military reasons supported Clausewitz's assertions.

On May 8, the Poles besieged Kiev and drove Yegorov's Army from the city within days and back to the Dnieper River.[74] Pilsudski achieved victory using the same mobility, surprise, and deception tactics at Vilna. Using cavalry's superior mobility, the Poles cut off the Russian lines of communication by striking in the flanks and capturing rail and road intersections while infantry and artillery fixed the enemy at Kiev. By this time, French military observers, such as Major Charles De Gaulle, commented that the Poles had developed a highly fluid and well-defined form of warfare that best suited the capabilities of the Polish Army.[75] Thus, after Kiev, the Polish theory and doctrine began to coalesce with cavalry or mobile forces serving as the primary source of delivering swift combat power and achieving surprise and gaining the initiative. Unfortunately, the emergent theory and doctrine failed to incorporate a robust logistical infrastructure to support operations over vast distances and the Russians quickly exploited that weakness.

After Kiev, both armies reorganized and resupplied until June. Pilsudski went back to Warsaw in order to reconsider the strategic and operational problem to develop additional political and military options. There were concerns that the Russians in the Ukraine were not destroyed and too much of the Polish Army was dedicated toward defending the South and no longer available to fight Tukhachevsky.[76] Moreover, the English and French, and many within the Polish Parliament, demanded peace.[77] Believing time remained for political deliberation and an opportunity to end the war without further military action, the Poles ceded the initiative back to the Russians.

As feared, the Russians were far from defeated and took the initiative by conducting a counter-attack. In early June, the Polish Air Service spotted the First Cavalry Army under the

---

[74] Adam Zamoyski, *Warsaw 1920* (London: Harper Collins), 33.
[75] Ibid., 36.
[76] Ibid., 37.
[77] Elbert Farman, "The Polish-Bolshevik Cavalry Campaigns of 1920," *The Cavalry Journal* 30, no. 122 (January 1921): 224.

command of Semyon Budyonny, moving northwest toward Kiev. Budyonny tore through the Ukraine, crossed over 1,000 miles from the Caucasus Mountains, and bypassed defenses in order to cut the rail, telegraph, and other vital lines of communications supporting the Polish Army at Kiev. By mid June, the Poles were unable to retain Kiev and retreated hundreds of miles back to the Bug River and the city of Lwow.[78]

The situation in the north unfolded in a similar fashion. The Polish First, Fourth and Seventh Armies, under the command of Stanislaw Szeptycki, had the task of preventing the Russians pouring out of the White Ruthenian Gate and controlling Belorussia. With the Fourth arrayed along the Berezina River and the Seventh operating as the strategic reserve, Szeptycki maneuvered to fix the Russian forces with an area defense while waiting for Pilsudski's forces that never arrived. In response to Szeptycki, the Russians maneuvered their Fourth, Fifteenth, and Third Armies through a narrow corridor along the Dvina River and created a breakthrough in the dispersed Polish defensive line. With the line broken, Russian cavalry interdicted lines of communication and isolated several Polish divisions and forced them to conduct a hasty retreat back to Vilna and beyond.[79]

By August, foreign newspapers reported Russian forces 75 miles from Warsaw and laying siege to the fortresses of Lomza and Brest-Litovsk along the Bug River.[80] Like Pilsudski's drive toward in the Ukraine, Tukhachevsky advanced with rapid speed, but overextended his lines of communication and isolated his main force from his operational reserve. It was a risk Tukhachevsky accepted since it was necessary to maintain the initiative in order to defeat the Polish Army and capture Warsaw.

---

[78] Norman Davies, *White Eagle, Red Star* (London: Random House E-Books, 2003), under "Location 2246 Amazon Kindle," Pimlico Electronic Book Edition; and, Richard M. Watt, *Bitter Glory, Poland and its Fate 1918 to 1939* (New York: Simon and Schuster), 124; and, Elbert Farman, "The Polish-Bolshevik Cavalry Campaigns of 1920," *The Cavalry Journal* 30, no. 122 (January 1921): 228.
[79] Norman Davies, *White Eagle, Red Star* (London: Random House E-Books, 2003), under "Location 1581 Amazon Kindle," Pimlico Electronic Book Edition; and, Richard M. Watt, *Bitter Glory, Poland and its Fate 1918 to 1939* (New York: Simon and Schuster), 127-129.
[80] Anonymous, "Red Army Now 75 Miles from Warsaw," *The New York Times*, http://query.nytimes.com/mem/archive-free/pdf?res=F50D17F73A5511738DDDAB0894D0405B808EF1D3 (accessed January 15, 2012).

To defend Warsaw, Pilsudski and the High Command arrayed the Fifth, First, Second, Fourth, and Third armies from north to south along the Vistula River. Opposite the river were Tukhachevsky's Fourth, Fifteenth, Third, Sixteenth, and the Mozyr Group. Fortunately for the Poles, Yegorov failed to join Tukhachevsky in time to besiege Warsaw. While Tukhachevsky prepared and waited for Yegorov, Pilsudski struck first at Mozyr Group, the left flank of the Red Army. Pilsudski employed a well-developed Jominian tactic of turning the entire Russian opposition at the risk of his force becoming encircled. The gambit succeeded.[81]

The attack destroyed the Mozyr Group and not only turned Tukhachevksy's forces, but also created a breakthrough. With the collapse of the Mozyr Group and its remnants fleeing into the Sixteenth's sector, the left flank completely collapsed. Concerned that the Poles would envelope the entire Army of the Southwest, the Russian Third formed a new flank.[82] With the Russian line spreading thin, the Poles drove a wedge between the Russian Fourth and Fifteenth arrayed north of Warsaw and isolated both of them.[83] The net result of these actions was the defeat of Tukhachevsky's forces and Moscow suing for peace

The signing of the Treaty of Riga allowed the Poles to achieve an unexpected victory.[84] By 1921, Poland's borders virtually resembled those of 1772. The nation succeeded through bold military action and Pilsudski's ability to shape the diplomatic narrative in a way to sanction Poland's actions. In addition, after blending Jominian and Clausewitzian concepts, Pilsudski forged an emergent Polish theory and doctrine that centered on mobility, initiative, surprise, and deception. However, logistics remained a major weakness highlighted during the war and

---

[81] Richard M. Watt, *Bitter Glory, Poland and its Fate 1918 to 1939* (New York: Simon and Schuster), 116; and, Viscount D'Abernon, *The Eighteenth Decisive Battle of the World* (London: Hodder and Stoughton), 142; and, Harold Worrell, "The Battle of Warsaw, 1920: Impact on Operational Thought", Combined Arms Research Digital Library, *School of Advanced Military Studies Monograph* (1994), http://cgsc.cdmhost.com/cdm4/item_viewer.php?CISOROOT=/p4013coll3&CISOPTR=1325 (accessed January 13, 2012).
[82] Richard M. Watt, *Bitter Glory, Poland and its Fate 1918 to 1939* (New York: Simon and Schuster), 147.
[83] Viscount D'Abernon, *The Eighteenth Decisive Battle of the World* (London: Hodder and Stoughton), 148.
[84] Ann Cardwell, *Poland and Russia: The Last Quarter Century* (New York: Sheed and Ward, 1944), 12.

continued to hinder military operations in subsequent years because the Polish industrial

infrastructure was virtually non-existent given Poland's position as an agrarian society.

After the war, Pilsudski retired from public life and Poland focused inward on

establishing a new government. The problems facing the establishment of a new government

were enormous and ranged from consolidating over 20 political parties, redistributing wealth, and

building an export capacity. In the late eighteenth century, Poland was a food-exporting nation.

However, by the early 1920s, less than 30 percent of the land was arable, private citizens had

little money to cultivate the fields, and Germany and Russia heavily taxed Polish imports.

Between 1918 and 1922, at least six different governments formed to solve Poland's problems

with little success. To stay economically solvent, the Poles borrowed heavily from the French,

British, the Americans, and printed trillions of Polish marks. The result was high inflation and an

intolerable exchange rate of one United States dollar for every 120 marks. In this situation, the

Poles were in no position to build up their industrial base, let alone consider strengthening their

military.[85]

The Parliament averted to crisis mode. In 1923, the government elected Wladyslaw

Grabski, a political moderate not affiliated with any political party, because the consensus was he

was a financial genius. Leading the government and acting as the Minister of Finance, Grabski

put Poland on the gold standard and created the Bank of Poland. He also abolished the use of

multiple currencies, established the zloty as the standard currency, and established favored trade

nation status with France.[86]

By 1924, it appeared the national budget was balanced and developing into a surplus.

However, these estimates were based on projections of a positive farming season that turned

disastrous by the end of the year. In November 1925, amid ongoing trade disputes with Germany

---

[85] Roman Debicki, *Foreign Policy of Poland, 1919-1939* (New York: Praeger), 38, 260-262; and, Richard M. Watt, *Bitter Glory, Poland and its Fate 1918 to 1939* (New York: Simon and Schuster), 197.
[86] Adam Zamoyski, *The Polish Way* (New York: Hippocrene Books), 348; Robert Machray, *Poland 1914-1931,* (London: George Allen and Unwin Ltd), 265.

and the latter refusing to purchase coal from the Silesias region, Grabski resigned as the nation plunged back into economic chaos. Riots spread from Warsaw to Krakow.[87] Many non-ethnic Poles and non-Catholics were severely beaten, persecuted, and accused of causing the economic crisis. Amidst the crisis, the Parliament prepared legislation to cut the national army to a few thousand men.[88]

The conservative right wing within Parliament moved quickly to re-establish control after Grabski's resignation. Led by Wincenty Witos of the Polish People's Party, the conservatives proposed revising the constitution in order to strengthen the powers of the Prime Minister, alter electoral law for Parliament members and extend their political authorities, and revise the judicial system.[89] In short, the new terms called for a new social order dominated by Catholic Poles not unlike the agenda championed by the Bar Confederation in the late 1760s. With the country facing economic collapse, social chaos, and a weak military, Pilsudski staged a coup.[90]

Applying the DIME model during this time-period again demonstrates Poland's tendency to use military force in order to pursue its strategic imperatives. Within a year of becoming a new nation, Poland entered into border disputes with the Germans, fought a brief war with the Ukrainians to seize their territory, and also found itself in a war for survival against the Russians. Again, Poland was willing to pursue its ambitions without garnering initial diplomatic support, delivering a compelling narrative across Europe, or biding time and devoting precious resources toward the economy. Simply put, Pilsudski's army pulled off a miracle against the Russians, but the underlying problems surrounding Poland resurfaced after Pilsudski retired from public service. The problems grew into social and economic chaos that eroded Poland's temporary

---

[87] Ferdynand Zweig, *Poland Between Two Wars* (London: Secker and Warburg), 47.
[88] Grace Humphrey, *Pilsudski: Builder of Poland* (New York, Scott and More), 250
[89] Ferdynand Zweig, *Poland Between Two Wars* (London: Secker and Warburg), 47-48.
[90] Ibid., 47.

ascendancy as a peer competitor with Russia in Eastern Europe. To quell the chaos, Pilsudski used military forces to stage his coup in 1926.[91]

Section IV. 1926-1935: Pilsudski's Coup to Pilsudski's Death

The period between 1926 and 1935, was marked by significant political and economic upheaval across Europe, ranging from the threat of communist expansion, the rise of Adolf Hitler in Germany, and the Great Depression. Most significantly, Pilsudski's struggled to maintain the Polish strategic imperative with a strong military, while building an industrial economy. In all his efforts, Pilsudski championed the victory over the Russians in 1920 and weaved the primacy of Polish military might into his narrative.[92] Yet, by the middle of the decade, Poland's superior strategic position, vis-à-vis Russia and Germany, collapsed, and the military became obsolete against the rise of the Nazi war machine.

The Strategic Environment between 1926-1935: Pilsudski's Coup to Pilsudski's Death

The Polish strategic imperative in the mid 1920s maintained the focus on establishing regional dominance, but those in Pilsudski's inner circle understood such an imperative required a holistic approach using all aspects of DIME. The specific tasks for Poland were to repair its fractured political framework, shift its reputation from an individualistic militarist state to one willing to participate in the broader interests of Europe, and to build the economy. Meanwhile, Russia remained Poland's existential threat. In turn, Poland appealed to the French to provide economic aid, military assistance and training in peace and combat forces in the event of war.[93] The tendency to rely on the French caused Poland to acquiesce on several points related to border disputes with Germany and fully indoctrinated the Polish Army into the French military tradition of defensive firepower and fortification. In time, Poland grew disenchanted with placating

---

[91] Ferdynand Zweig, *Poland Between Two Wars* (London: Secker and Warburg), 47-50.
[92] Richard Overy, *1939, Countdown to War* (New York: Viking), 6.
[93] Richard Watt, *Bitter Glory. Poland and its Fate, 1918-1939* (New York: Simon and Schuster), 246.

Western Europe's strategic imperatives and forged separate non-aggression pacts with Germany and Russia.

The use of DIME between 1926-1935: Pilsudski's Coup to Pilsudski's Death

In the diplomatic and information realm, Pilsudski projected a narrative of being surrounded by enemies and Western Europe was responsible for Poland's fragile security situation by not clearly defining its borders after the First World War.[94] The French accepted Poland's position, albeit somewhat reluctantly. They lent diplomatic support within the League of Nations, provided loans to invigorate the Polish economy, and maintained the Franco-Polish military alliance re-initiated in1921. However, systemic of an alliance with the French, and a stipulation for future support, France compelled Pilsudski to enter Poland into collective security agreements that placed Poland's security secondary to the strategic imperatives of Western Europe.

Moreover, despite French sponsorship, Poland was not a major power in dictating the course of broader European security affairs because of its isolation in Europe, weak economy, and militaristic reputation. Therefore, when the League of Nations advocated for a softening of economic constraints toward Germany in 1925, Poland had no choice but to support measures, such as the Locarno Pact, in order to keep investments and military assistance flowing.[95] Unfortunately, the Locarno Pact cost the nation its security position with Germany and Russia.

The Locarno Pact's purpose was to thwart communist expansion, normalize relations with Germany, and achieve post-war territorial settlements with new nations created after the First World War.[96] The normalization of Germany brought the nation back into the fold and replaced Poland as the vanguard against communist expansion. With Germany re-integrated, Europe, especially France, relied less on a strong Polish military for security. Consequently, by

---

[94] Richard Watt, *Bitter Glory. Poland and its Fate, 1918-1939* (New York: Simon and Schuster), 246-248.
[95] Roman Debicki, *Foreign Policy of Poland, 1919-1939* (New York: Frederick A. Praeger), 57.
[96] Norman Davies, *God's Playground, a History of Poland, 1795 to the Present* (New York: Columbia University Press), 501.

the end of the decade, the French military mission to Poland dwindled with no definitive guarantee of sending military forces in the event of war.

As mentioned, the Locarno Pact also attempted to achieve post-war territorial settlements with new nations after the First World War. With respect to the question of the German-Polish border and access to the sea and port city of Danzig, the Pact required Germany and Poland to allow a League of Nations tribunal to arbitrate disputes.[97] Even after the signatories ratified the Pact, the German-Polish border remained a contentious issue and both sides conducted a low intensity, undeclared state of war, and engaged in political subversion to influence plebiscite self-determination in regions that harbored vast deposits of industrial raw materials.[98]

In time, Poland grew restless in supporting the broader strategic imperatives within Europe and Pilsudski attempted to achieve Poland's strategic imperative of regional dominance by engaging with Eastern European nations. Four years after the signing of the Locarno Pact, Pilsudski achieved diplomatic success with the Litvinov Protocol. The protocol provided the basis for a long-term Polish-Soviet non-aggression pact formally signed in 1932. The principle benefits of a non-aggression pact with Russia are that it gave Poland time to build its military and economy. Coinciding with the pact with Russia, Poland forged a military alliance with Romania in 1926. The purpose of the arrangement was to protect both nations against the event of German and Hungarian hostilities against Romania and a Russian invasion against Poland.[99]

Adolf Hitler's rise to power in Germany dismantled the collective security framework in Europe and sent nations on the road to war.[100] Hitler was diplomatically adept in assuming Germany was at the strategic center of security in Europe. Within a year of assuming the

---

[97] "Locarno Treaty," October 16, 1925, League of Nations Treaty Series 54, no. 1295, pt. 1,2 (1926): 329-39.

[98] Samuel L. Sharp, *Poland. White Eagle on a Red Field* (Cambridge: Harvard University Press), 131-135.

[99] Richard Watt, *Bitter Glory. Poland and its Fate, 1918-1939* (New York: Simon and Schuster), 262-264; and, Roman Debicki, *Foreign Policy of Poland, 1919-1939* (New York: Frederick A. Praeger), 61, 139-142.

[100] Peter Paret, *Makers of Modern Strategy, from Machiavelli to the Nuclear Age* (Princeton, Princeton University Press), 491.

Chancellery in 1933, Hitler withdrew Germany from the League of Nations and announced the re-armament of the military.[101] In essence, the security provided by the Locarno Pact, and similar treaties collapsed, forcing Western Europe to form separate security agreements with and against Germany.

Sensing war-weariness and lacking the diplomatic and economic means to oppose him, Hitler tested Europe's resolve in upholding German obligations under the Treaty of Versailles. In a counterblow to the Locarno Pact, Hitler sought to build a Central and Eastern Europe alliance to challenge Western Europe. Moreover, like Napoleon, Hitler viewed an alliance with Poland as a matter of convenience. Pacifying Poland in the short term allowed Hitler to obtain political concessions from Western Europe without the fear of an attack. Thus, Germany's political discourse in Poland culminated in the signing of a German-Polish Non-Aggression Pact in 1934.[102] With Poland placated, and fresh from agreeing to a ten-year extension of a pre-existing economic German-Soviet Pact from 1922, Hitler turned his attention toward building the Nazi war machine.[103] Meanwhile, despite maintaining a separate non-aggression pact with Russia, the Polish military refined their war planning efforts in case of a Russian invasion.

After defeating the Russians in the early 1920s, Poland's military embraced the principles established by Ferdinand Foch's victorious French army from the First World War.[104] To a lesser degree, the military used emerging theory from the British. In particular, J.F.C. Fuller's concept of using masses of light tanks, and Liddell Hart's notions of limited war, informed senior officers of how to use emerging mobile capabilities.[105] However, the French military assistance mission and Foch's prestige swayed the Poles into adopting a defensive theory of war in planning a military contest against the Russians.

---

[101] Peter Paret, *Makers of Modern Strategy, from Machiavelli to the Nuclear Age* (Princeton, Princeton University Press), 491-493.

[102] Adam Zamoyski, *The Polish Way, a Thousand Year History of the Poles and their Culture* (New York: Hippocrene Books), 354.

[103] Roman Debicki, *Foreign Policy of Poland, 1919-1939* (New York: Frederick A. Praeger), 79.

[104] Piotr Wandycz, *France and her Eastern Allies* (Minneapolis: University of Minnesota Press), 214.

[105] James Corum, *The Roots of Blitzkrieg* (Lawrence: University of Kansas Press), 143.

Foch traveled to Poland during the 1920s and advocated that overwhelming defensive firepower from artillery enabled the infantry to win battles. Further, Foch contended that new technology, such as tanks, armored cars, and aircraft were means to augment the infantry and not to operate independently in order to achieve separate tactical objectives.[106] In addition, natural terrain obstacles, such as mountains and rivers, combined with a complex fortress system, enabled the infantry to fight from prepared positions on terrain of their choosing. What is interesting to point out is that during this time, as the Poles drew closer to the French tradition, they departed from their emergent theory and doctrine based on mobility, initiative, surprise, and deception that enabled victory against the Russians.

As the Poles trained in the French tradition, they believed that while Germany was contained under the constraints of the Treaty of Versailles, and the Rhineland occupied, most of the war planning should focus on repelling a Soviet invasion. Military planners realized fighting the communists proved a difficult operational and tactical problem to solve due to limited logistics, mechanization, and the presence of restricted terrain across the Eastern frontier. To repel the Soviets, the Poles developed the East Plan, or referred to as Plan Wschod.

The East Plan's operational approach was to initially delay or disrupt the committed Soviet forces crossing the Dnieper River before falling back to defensive positions along the Polish border. It also relied on a military pact with Romania and built upon Plan Foch developed in 1923. The plan assumed that since most of the eastern frontier was agrarian, lacked sufficient rail and roads, possessed restrictive terrain, the Soviets would split armies into groups and take time to mobilize. However, intelligence estimated the Soviets would mobilize up to 70 divisions

---

[106] David Mets and Harold Winton, *The Challenge of Change. Military Institutions and New Realities, 1918-1941* (Lincoln: University of Nebraska Press), 18.

within a month of hostilities. Moreover, the plan assumed the Soviets would attempt to converge on Warsaw, the operational center of gravity, as demonstrated in 1920.[107]

To repel the invasion, the Poles created six army groups arrayed from Latvia in the north to Romania in the south and relied on additional divisions promised by the Romanians under the provisions of a 1926 treaty between the two nations. In total, the Poles planned to mobilize up to 39 active and reserve infantry divisions, three national defense brigades, three cavalry divisions, and an assorted mix of cavalry and light mixed divisions. The Reserve Army maintained the flexibility to move either north or south while based outside Warsaw. Unfortunately, the East Plan contained at least two major flaws.[108]

First, the plan over-relied on a static and prepared defense because of the lack of mechanization within the Polish Army. Fighting in the east required a highly mobile and mechanized army with overwhelming offensive firepower, but the Poles had invested very little in aircraft and armor because analysis of the Eastern Theater led the Polish High Command to believe the marshy terrain was ill suited for mechanized forces.[109] Consequently, the Poles relied on trenches, fortifications, and defensive firepower from artillery.

Lack of mobility led to a semi-fixed defensive force that that tried to hold a long defensive perimeter, concentrated in regions, while it relied on cavalry to conduct offensive operations.[110] However, cavalry proved unable to strike at the Soviet operational reserve conceptualized under their emerging deep operations theory. In deep operations theory, the communists realized their source of military strength was dependent on a second wave of

---

[107] Steven Zaloga and Victor Madej, *The Polish Campaign 1939* (New York: Hippocrene Books, 1985), 15-18; David Mets and Harold Winton, *The Challenge of Change. Military Institutions and New Realities, 1918-1941* (Lincoln: University of Nebraska Press), 124.

[108] Steven Zaloga and Victor Madej, *The Polish Campaign 1939* (New York: Hippocrene Books, 1985), 8-16.

[109] Ibid., 18.

[110] David Williamson, *Poland Betrayed. The Nazi-Soviet Invasions of 1939* (Mechanicsburg: Stackpole Books), 21.

operational forces that could exploit a breakthrough in the Polish defensive lines and continue a swift attack to Warsaw via mobility and offensive firepower.[111]

The second flaw in the plan was that given the state of Polish logistics, the plan was not feasible. The Poles never solved the logistical shortfalls that hampered the Army after the recent war with the Russians. The main problems rested with how the High Command organized the Army within a network of regional commands with no centralized distribution network.[112] Essentially, each regional commander requisitioned their own supplies from their regional logistical hub. This worked during peacetime and if a division fought within its regional command, but unrealistic under Plan East that required distributed operations across hundreds of miles.

The disparity between the rail systems in the eastern half of Poland and the time it took to push supplies from the ports and Warsaw contributed to the logistical shortfall. Lack of improved rail and roads also negatively affected the ability to command and control multiple divisions across hundreds of miles. Since very few rail networks and roads existed to support the resupply of an army exceeding twenty divisions in Eastern Poland, the Army relied on horse-drawn logistics. Without access to timely resupply and in the amounts required, Plan East risked early culmination by military forces.[113]

The state of the Polish economic situation fared litter better than the military plan. For a time, the early economic conditions led to the rapid modernization of the Polish military, but later, the economy led to the military's demise. Fundamentally, in order for Poland to achieve its strategic aim and execute a successful military operation, it required a robust economy and a swift modernization policy to convert from an agrarian to industrial export economy. Due to foreign

---

[111] Richard Harrison, *Architect of Soviet Victory in World War II. The Life and Theories of G.S. Isserson,* (Jefferson: McFarland & Company, Inc., Publishers), 77.

[112] David Williamson, *Poland Betrayed. The Nazi-Soviet Invasions of 1939* (Mechanicsburg: Stackpole Books), 19.

[113] David Williamson, *Poland Betrayed. The Nazi-Soviet Invasions of 1939* (Mechanicsburg: Stackpole Books), 25-28; Mieczyslaw Neugebauer, *The Defence of Poland, September 1939* (London: M. I. Kolin), 203.

occupation, Poland largely missed the advent of the industrial revolution in Europe during the eighteenth and nineteenth centuries. What little industrialization that existed represented a patchwork of development in various pockets across Western and Southern Poland, in areas such as Upper Silesia and along the shared border with Czechoslovakia.[114] Consequently, Poland's economy was still agrarian in the 1920s.

When the economy crashed in 1925, Poland sought to diversify its economy via the development of an aggressive industrial program.[115] Under the guidance of Charles Dewey and Edward Kemmerer from the United States, Poland obtained a stabilization loan. The loan's purpose was to curtail the zloty's rampant inflation and to modernize its industrial capacity by focusing on an area known as the Polish Industrial Triangle.[116] The loan achieved its purpose.

In time, foreign investments in the Polish Industrial Triangle exceeded the sum of 72 million American dollars and the Poles enjoyed trade surpluses through exportation of coal to Western Europe due to a shortage of the commodity from other sources. Between 1926 and 1930, one third of the economy was industrial based. Consequently, the military expanded. Similar to Prussia's economic expansion in the prior century an investment in railroads and ports, Poland built up its industrial capacity while keeping its dual use by the military in mind. For example, the tiny fishing village of Gdynia on the Baltic transformed into Poland's true commercial and military port. Gdynia also reduced the reliance on the contested port of Danzig.[117]

The economic reforms enabled Poland to enjoy a robust economy by the end of the 1920s and the nation stood to prosper in the next decade. However, the global effects of the Great Depression devastated the Polish economy. By 1933, the budget reflected a 77 million zloty shortfall compared to the 2.8 billion surplus enjoyed in 1929.[118] In sum, the Great Depression hit

---

[114] Oscar Halecki, *a History of Polan* (New York: Dorset Press), 293.

[115] Grace Humphrey, *Pilsudski* (New York: Scot and More), 267.

[116] Roman Debicki, *Foreign Policy of Poland, 1919-1939* (New York: Frederick A. Praeger), 57.

[117] Robert Machray, *Poland, 1914-1931* (London: George Allen and Unwin), 342; Geoffrey Wawro, *The Franco-Prussian War* (Cambridge: Cambridge University Press), 49, 309;

[118] Geoffrey Wawro, *The Franco-Prussian War* (Cambridge: Cambridge University Press), 420-423.

Poland in 1930 and lingered through 1935.[119] With such a significant impact to the economy that still required international loans to function, Poland curtailed its military modernization program and never developed the mechanized forces necessary to execute Plan East. Further, the military it fielded against Germany in 1939 was at least four years out of date and the bulk of its forces were purchased from 1926-1933.

The Great Depression not only shattered Poland's ability to invest in its military after 1933, but also weakened Western Europe's position in requiring Germany to pay war reparations and other stipulations mandated by the Treaty of Versailles. As Western Europe sought to raise capital to pay off their own war debts, nations agreed to relax Germany's obligation during the Lausanne Conference in 1932.[120] The net result of the Lausanne Conference was that it allowed Germany to recover from the Great Depression and reinvigorate its economy at a much faster rate than most of Europe.

While Germany and Western Europe suffered through the Great Depression, Joseph Stalin successfully launched his First Five Year Plan in order to industrialize the Soviet Union. As the Soviet economy improved at a rate exceeding most of Europe, the Germans and Soviets conducted military exchanges until Hitler and the Nazi regime took power. By the mid 1930s, after most European nations had weathered the worst effects of the Great Depression and Germany and the Soviet Union accelerated their industrial modernization programs. This led to both nations adopting military mechanization.[121]

Poland's use of DIME during the middle of the interwar period to achieve its strategic imperative of regional dominance met with mixed results. While initially militarily superior Russia, Poland lacked the diplomatic, information, and economic acumen in order to safeguard its

---

[119] Ferdynand Zweig, *Poland Between Two Wars* (London: Secker and Warburg), 167.

[120] United States Holocaust Memorial Museum, "German Prewar Expansion," Holocaust Encyclopedia, http://www.ushmm.org/wlc/en/article.php?ModuleId=10005439 (accessed January 16, 2012).

[121] Robert Conquest, *The Great Terror, a Reassessment* (Oxford: Oxford University Press), 18; Richard J. Evans, *The Coming of the Third Reich* (New York: Penguin Press), 99, 445.

strategic interests when entering to the broader collective security framework sponsored by France. Thus, Poland turned to its neighbors in Central and Eastern Europe and forged separate non-aggression pacts with Germany and Russia. Poland also gained Romania as a military ally.

The non-aggression pacts led to temporary peace that would have granted time to build a stronger military and industrial economy, but the Great Depression shattered Poland's ability to achieve its strategic imperative during Pilsudski's final years. With a ravaged economy and an obsolete military, Poland began to perceive Germany as the existential threat to its sovereignty. Thus, the country hastily attempted to strengthen its military forces using an obsolete defensive theory and doctrine and would do so without its military leader. In 1935, Jozef Pilsudski died and his successors struggled to govern in the wake of his legacy.

Section V. 1936-1939: Rise of the Nazi War Machine to Poland's Failure

The waning years of the 1930s reflected the rise of the Nazi war machine and the Poles using their military to defend their sovereignty. By 1936, as Hitler gained power and influence, the Polish High Command shifted their military planning efforts to Germany. When the threat of war drew closer, Poland found itself isolated from Europe because they possessed few strategic incentives to offer potential allies for stopping the military advance of Hitler. Ironically, this is the same scenario that plagued King Poniatowski back in the eighteenth century and forced him to abandon his strategic imperatives. Thus, the continuity of Poland using military means as the primary way of achieving their strategic imperatives yielded the same results dating back to the eighteenth century. Like the old Polish-Lithuanian Commonwealth, the price for using principally military means resulted in the destruction of Poland in 1939.

The Strategic Environment between 1936-1939: Rise of the Nazi War Machine to Poland's Failure

Since 1919, Western European military forces had occupied the Rhineland in order to secure the region as a buffer against Germany. While supposed to remain until 1936, they departed in 1930. This decision was part of a larger reconciliation effort that traced its roots back to the Great Depression and the growing unwillingness to spend money on the rearmament of Europe. War weary and lacking political will, Western Europe preferred appeasement over war. Thus, the German Wehrmacht occupied the Rhineland in 1936 unopposed. Germany continued to exploit Western Europe's passiveness by annexing Austria, and occupying more territory that mainly ended with Czechoslovakia in early1939. With each action, Germany grew bolder in its demands toward Poland by requiring the nation to yield contested territory. Without allies willing to oppose Germany with force, Poland found itself in a position of strategic disadvantage in preparing for war against Germany.[122]

The use of DIME between 1936-1939: Rise of the Nazi War Machine to Poland's Failure

As discussed, since the end of the First World War, the German-Polish border remained a contentious issue. For over a decade, Germans found themselves living in the new Poland and Poles enjoyed access to the sea through a narrow passage that isolated Prussia from Germany. Moreover, by building a second port city at Gdynia, Poland threated control of the sea lanes within the immediate vicinity of Danzig.[123] While the border tensions reached temporary calmness through a series of economic agreements, the underlying causes remained. When Hitler came to power in 1933, he vowed to resolve the tensions.

---

[122] Joseph Miranda, "The Rhineland War: What if World War II Started in 1936?" *World at War*, January 2011, 6-8; John Keegan, *The Second World War* (New York: Penguin Books), 36-41.
[123] Joseph Miranda, "The Rhineland War: What is World War II Started in 1936?" *World at War*, January 2011, 7.

Hitler demanded that the Poles cede back all the lands in former German territories granted by the Treaty of Versailles and the Paris Peace Conference.[124] With the possibility of war, the Poles turned their nation's military capacity toward defending against Germany. Diplomatically, Poland stated they would stand up to Hitler alone, if necessary, and appealed to Western Europe to aid in their struggle against a perceived infringement upon their sovereignty.[125] In truth, the Poles were never willing to seek a diplomatic solution and openly prepared their military for war.

According to Sir Edmond Ironside, a British general visiting Poland, he remarked that Poland had full confidence in its military to defeat the Germans. In fact, with the victory over the Russians in 1920 still fresh in their minds, the Ironside remarked that the Poles possessed a mad spirit of optimism and harbored no thoughts of diplomatically resolving their problems with the Germans.[126] Unfortunately, as the threat of war loomed closer, Polish hubris failed to gain definitive assurances from Europe for military assistance with the exception of an unclear British Guarantee of protection in 1939.[127] Without allies, Poland set to the task of preparing their military for war, but lacked the means to fight the Nazis.

Outside of some early planning efforts against the Germans in the 1920s, the Poles never considered war with Germany a real possibility. Most of their war planning efforts had focused on the Russians. However, rather than consider simply the Russians, or the Germans, the Polish High Command needed to develop a plan to fight a two-front war against both nations. While the benefit of historical hindsight makes this assertion seem an obvious statement, and perhaps an unfair judgment, a two-front war always represented the worse case scenario and had occurred at least three times in Poland's relatively recent history.

---

[124] Mathew Cooper, *The German Army, 1933-1945* (Lanham: Scarborough House Publishers), 107.
[125] The Avalon Project, *Munich Pact, September 29, 1938,* http://avalon.law.yale.edu/imt/munich1.asp (accessed January 10, 2012).
[126] Richard Overy, *1939, Countdown to War* (New York: Viking), 15.
[127] Ibid., 12-16.

At one time Poland had considered the possibility of a two-front war, but abandoned it when Pilsudski took power in 1926. The basis for abandoning a two-front contingency was in no small part related to Pilsudski's hatred of the Russians, the belief in a sizable French military contribution to open a second front, and the perceived containment of Germany by Western Europe. This logic represented a diplomatic failure and Pilsudski never seriously considered the historical precedence for a potential Nazi-Soviet alliance and war against Poland.[128]

With the thought of fighting the Germans in the forefront of military planning efforts, the High Command began drafting Plan West, or Plan Zachod. Plan West planning efforts formally began after Hitler occupied the Rhineland. In writing the plan, French military theory and doctrine dominated.[129] Later, after the annexation of Austria and eventual fall of Czechoslovakia, the High Command conducted a modern form of crisis action planning from March through September of 1939 in order to refine Plan West and prepare for the perceived German threat coming out of East Prussia and Czechoslovakia.[130]

The overall assessment of Plan West, initially conducted in 1936 by a Polish General Inspectorate study, indicated the mechanization of the Wehrmacht presented significant operational and tactical challenges.[131] Moreover, the study grimly indicated that without further loans to secure Polish mechanized forces, aircraft, and additional ships, Germany would prevail in a war within a couple of months.[132] Unfortunately, during the years of budget surplus before the Great Depression, Poland chose to invest in a navy and the industrial triangle versus mechanization. The reasons for this are varied. The navy served as a source of national pride, and

[128] Samuel L. Sharp, *Poland. White Eagle on a Red Field* (Cambridge: Harvard University Press), 148; and, David Williamson, *Poland Betrayed, The Nazi-Soviet Invasions of 1939* (Mechanicsburg, Stackpole Books), 48; and, Grace Humphrey, *Pilsudski* (New York: Scott and More), 264; Gaynor Johnson, *Locarno Revisited, European Diplomacy, 1920-1929* (New York: Routledge), 90.
[129] Joseph Miranda, "The Rhineland War: What if World War II Started in 1936?," *World at War,* December 2011, 6.
[130] David Williamson, *Poland Betrayed. The Nazi-Soviet Invasions of 1939* (Mechanicsburg: Stackpole Books), 48.
[131] Norman Davis, *God's Playground, a History of Poland. 1795 to the Present* (New York: Columbia University Press), 430.
[132] Ibid., 430-433.

as stated before, the High Command believed the greatest threat came from Russia. Therefore, they assumed risk by building a military capable of conducting defensive and not offensive operations in the Eastern Theater. Thus, when the study pointed out the glaring lack of Polish mechanization, Poland possessed little means in order to remedy the shortfall and given their hubris, the Poles chose a military solution to confront Hitler in lieu of diplomacy.

Following French doctrine and theory, the Polish military fully matured in the 1930s. The Army designated the infantry division as its principle warfighting element. Since 1936, Poland drafted 1.5 million reservists and national guardsmen to augment the active military force and integrated the reservists into the professional military training and education system. Plan West assumed the initial fielding of at least 283,000 troops. After mobilization, Poled planned to field a total of 2.5 million men. In sum, the Poles planned to fight with 30 infantry divisions, 11 cavalry brigades, and additional reserve forces.[133]

Each infantry division was organized under regional armies and consisted of separate artillery and cavalry units. The army continued to employ the French 75mm artillery cannon as its mainstay defensive firepower weapon. The cavalry battalions functioned as dismounted infantry units and were equipped with anti-tank weapons. For armor, the Poles had replaced many of the outdated Renault FT-17s with the Polish built TK-3 and TKS tankettes, and the 7TP light tank. However, none of the armor was utilized for separate offensive maneuvers. In addition to ground forces, Plan West contained air force and naval capabilities.[134]

The Air Force had 78 combat squadrons, consisting of fighters, interceptors, bombers, and observers, but compared to the German Luftwaffe, were a legacy force.[135] Of the 688 aircraft in service, only the P-11C fighter and P-37B bomber provided the means to conduct offensive

---

[133] David Williamson, *Poland Betrayed, The Nazi-Soviet Invasions of 1939* (Mechanicsburg, Stackpole Books), 19-21, 120-123; and, Steven Zaloga, *The Polish Army, 1939-1945* (Oxford: Osprey Publishing), 5.
[134] Jonasz, Maciej, "The State of the Polish Military in 1939" *World at War*, December 2010, 39; and, Steven Zaloga, *Poland 1939. The Birth of Blitzkrieg* (Oxford: Osprey Publishing), 28.
[135] David Williamson, *Poland Betrayed, The Nazi-Soviet Invasions of 1939* (Mechanicsburg, Stackpole Books), 24.

counter air against the Messerschmitt Bf-110 fighter-bomber and fielded German forces.[136] In addition, the High Command never integrated the Polish Air Force with ground forces the same way the German General Staff used the Luftwaffe to support the maneuver of the Wehrmacht. The Navy also operated as a separate force with separate tactical objectives.

The Polish Navy had two major components. The first, the Riverine Flotilla, was a river force composed of gunboats that protected major river systems and the Pripyet Marsh region along the Eastern Frontier. The principle utility behind the gunboats was to augment the infantry against the Soviets and to provide logistical supplies to areas deemed impassable by rail or road. The second component, based in Gdynia, was the blue-water navy. The main force consisted of destroyers, submarines, and several minesweepers supported by coastal defense batteries. Unfortunately, the navy provided no operational or tactical advantage. Its close proximity to Danzig by a mere 20 miles kept it under constant fire by the Germans and easily within range of the Luftwaffe. Hence, the Navy was more suited toward operating in the Baltic in order to protect shipping, but operating in the open water put the Navy at risk from the combined fleets of Germany and the Soviet Union.[137]

As with the Plan East, the lack of mechanization and limited lines of communications greatly affected Poland's operational reach and ability to maintain a high operations tempo from Warsaw to the assessed invasion avenues of approach. To minimize the operational reach and tempo limitations, the High Command organized the Army into regional districts and each district was responsible for garnering the necessary logistical requirements of their armies.[138] However, if individual armies became isolated or bypassed, Warsaw had little means of resupplying the them. Therefore, the High Command preferred a defense concentrated in Central Poland that arrayed

[136] David Stone, *Hitler's Army, the Men, Machines, and Organization 1939-1945* (Minneapolis: Zenith Press), 272.

[137] Polish Navy Portal, *1939-1947, Polish Navy Homepage*, http://www.polishnavy.pl/PMW/history/index_03.html (accessed November 14, 2011); Michael Peszke, *Poland's Navy, 1918-1945*, (New York: Hippocrene Books), 33,202.

[138] Mieczyslaw Norwid-Neugebauer, *the Defence of Poland, 1939* (Charlottesville: University of Virginia), 202.

forces along a series of defensive regions that were designed to absorb the opening German offensive thrusts, protect Warsaw, and provide time for mobilization.[139]

The High Command believed that the initial defensive belt approach for Plan West was feasible but it ceded initiative and key terrain to the Germans during the opening hours of the war. The Polish government preferred delivering a decisive military blow to the Germans and denying them Danzig and the Polish Corridor. However, the military lacked the means to fully mobilize and maneuver to meet the opposition before Germany seized key terrain.[140] Therefore, the High Command reached a compromise, and the bulk of forces concentrated in the Central and Western regions of Poland and within the Polish Corridor. Additionally, a token force guarded the Eastern Frontier.[141] The operational reserve resided in vicinity of Warsaw.

In addition to organizing the army within regions, the High Command assumed the cavalry could achieve operational reach and tempo in order to achieve limited objectives related to disrupting German lines of communication.[142] This approach was similar to the one employed in 1920 against the Soviets. However, the General Staff had no appreciation for the speed and firepower the German Panzer divisions would enjoy across the flat plains of Poland. In addition to cavalry, the High Command adopted a half-hearted belief that the Polish Navy would slow the arrival of German troops to Danzig while the Air Force interdicted behind the front lines.[143]

In the end, Plan West assumed that established defensive regions allowed time to defend Poland until the French opened a second front. The High Command calculated the French would provide military support within two weeks of hostilities based on previous military exchanges

---

[139] Henryk Sololowski, *German Invasion of Poland During WW2*, Polish Combatants' Associate Website, http://felsztyn.tripod.com/germaninvasion/id11.html (accessed December 13, 2011).
[140] David Williamson, *Poland Betrayed, The Nazi-Soviet Invasions of 1939* (Mechanicsburg, Stackpole Books), 55.
[141] Henryk Sololowski, *German Invasion of Poland During WW2*, Polish Combatants' Associate Website, http://felsztyn.tripod.com/germaninvasion/id11.html (accessed January 7, 2012).
Polish Navy Portal, *1939-1947, Polish Navy Homepage*, http://www.polishnavy.pl/PMW/history/index_03.html (accessed November 17, 2011).
[142] Steve Zaloga and W. Victor Madej, *the Polish Campaign, 1939* (New York: Hippocrene Books), 37.
[143] Ibid., 28-31.

with the French during the long-standing military assistance mission to Poland.[144] However, the French never allocated specific military forces during crisis action planning in 1939. Therefore, with faulty assumptions, the High Command believed that while they lacked mechanization, the Polish military possessed the means to delay the capture of Warsaw and initiate a counter-attack with French assistance. Thus, the Poles spent the waning summer months of 1939 in a false sense of security.

The events that unfolded between September 1 and October 6, 1939, formed the opening chapter of the Second World War. In a brilliant display of maneuver warfare and combined arms, Germany opened hostilities across three axis, deploying forces against the Polish Corridor, Lodz, and Krakow simultaneously.[145] Within days, the German Luftwaffe decimated the Polish Air Force. Against the Polish Army, the Luftwaffe either fixed units in place for destruction by German combined arms maneuver forces, or rendered their withdrawal along the defensive regions impossible. As a consequence of the rapid German advance, Polish lines of communication became saturated with civilians and unable to support the army.[146] Additionally, the Polish Navy proved ineffective and fled into open water for Great Britain.

Despite setbacks, the Poles fought on, waiting for the French, and expecting them to arrive by mid-September. Instead, the Poles were greeted by the unanticipated arrival of the Soviet Army on September 18th. The emergence of a fresh army and the opening of a second front made the defense of Poland impossible. The French never arrived and Poland fell on October 6th (see Figure 6). Thousands with the Polish military escaped capture and reformed in France and Britain. Later, in 1941, when Russia signed the Polish-Soviet Agreement in 1941 with Great Britain, thousands of prisoners were released to form the Polish Second Corps after surviving the gulags of Siberia. These former prisoners filled a requirement to replenish the front lines by providing the Allies additional means to fight in places, such as North Africa and Italy,

---

[144] Richard Overy, *1939. Countdown to War* (New York: Viking), 10.
[145] Steven Zaloga, *The Polish Army, 1939-1945* (Oxford: Osprey Publishing), 8.
[146] Ibid., 10.

and gave the exiled Polish government the false impression of fighting for the liberation of

Poland.[147] In total, and even after initial defeat, the Poles continued to field the fourth largest

Allied Army in Europe during the war and fought in the skies over Europe. Unfortunately, at

war's end, Poland served as a political token to obtain peace with the Soviet Union. It would take

another fifty years and the collapse of the Soviet Union before Poland regained its complete

independence.[148]

Section VI. Conclusions and Implications

This monograph made the assertion that Poland's demise in 1939 was a result of pursuing

centuries-old strategic imperatives of independence from Russia and regional dominance.[150]

Moreover, by using the DIME methodology, the conclusions at the end of each time-period

resulted in supporting the assertion that Poland predominantly used military means as the way of

---

[147] Oscar Halecki, *A History of Poland* (New York: Roy Publishers), 320-322.

[148] Norman Davies, *No Simple Victory. World War II in Europe, 1939-1945* (New York: Penguin Group), 78; Steven Zaloga, *The Polish Army, 1939-1945* (Oxford: Osprey Publishing), 6-14.

[149] U.S. Library of Congress, http://lcweb2.loc.gov/frd/cs/poland/pl01_05d.pdf (accessed January 5, 2012).

[150] W. Alison Phillips, *Poland* (New York: Henry Hold and Company), 66.

48

meeting its strategic imperatives. What became clear is that the Poles from 1764 to 1939 were fundamentally militant toward their neighbors and were willing to achieve their aims even if diplomatic, information, and economic means were not available to support the military.

By understanding the militant nature of the Poles, the answer to the primary research question became apparent. Poland's enduring strategic imperatives shaped its military and determined its use in1939 by requiring the military to adopt French military theory and doctrine while constantly being placed in a position of reacting to Poland's political authority without allies, control of the international discourse, or economic means to sustain modern forces. With this insight, readers have a better understanding of how strategic imperatives may shape and determine a nation's ways and means.

Analysis of the military and its role between the eighteenth and twentieth centuries revealed an interesting and unexpected finding. The author assumed that the lack of mechanization and defensive nature of the Polish military in 1939 was a direct result of the Franco-Polish military alliance dating back to the Duchy of Warsaw and multiple occupations by Russia. Therefore, it appeared that no opportunity existed for the development of a unique Polish way of war. However, by studying Pilsudski's military campaign against the Russians between 1919 and 1921, there was a brief, yet critical moment in Poland's military history to break with tradition and adopt a truly unique Polish theory and doctrine based on offensive firepower and maneuverability. Pilsudski's attempts to draw Tukhachevsky's Army south through an indirect approach of seizing territory in the Ukraine represented a clear example of Polish operational art during the interwar period.

Though the desired effects of Pilsudski's operational approach failed to materialize, Pilsudski continued the same approach when the Russians encircled Warsaw. Through a combination of Jominian tactics and Clausewitzian thought, Pilsudski managed to create a breakthrough in the Russian lines, repelling the invasion, and winning the war. Unfortunately, Poland's pursuit of its strategic imperatives without adequate diplomatic, information, and economic means endeared them to the French. As a result, the military trained and organized under the French tradition and abandoned a superior and emerging Polish military theory and doctrine.

Ultimately, Poland's military failure to defend the nation in 1939 is not attributed to a single military campaign, but more to a consistent historical miscalculation of the strategic environment and an enduring unwillingness to abstain from seeking regional dominance without sufficient means. Yet, this understanding does not detract from the commendable Polish plight. After a brief examination of the current Polish State, it appears pursuing strategic imperatives with mostly a military approach is over.

With respect to recommendations for further research, many potential opportunities exist. Perhaps the most advantageous is to continue the story of the evolution of the Polish military in the context of the Polish strategic imperatives from 1939 until the fall of communism. Examining this period will provide answers into how Poland managed to change and adopt a more holistic approach of using all of its instruments of national power.

Currently, Poland is a member of the European Union, the North Atlantic Treaty Organization, a major military contributor to the former Global War on Terror, and boasts an industrial-based economy. Unlike the Great Depression, its economy survived the global economic crisis in 2009 and its economy continues to expand. With a more holistic approach toward its strategic imperatives, Poland is now considered a valuable European ally by its neighbors and the United States. More importantly, it offers many strategic incentives for gaining and maintaining partnerships with other nations. For the first time in centuries, Poland has the means to pursue its strategic imperatives.

BIBLIOGRAPHY

BOOKS

PRIMARY SOURCES

Anonymous, "Red Army Now 75 Miles from Warsaw," The New York Times, http://query.nytimes.com/mem/archive-free/pdf?res=F50D17F73A5511738DDDAB0894D0405B808EF1D3 (accessed January 15, 2012).

Avalon Project. *Munich Pact, September 29, 1938.* 2008. http://avalon.law.yale.edu/imt/munich1.asp (accessed December 6, 2011).

Chlapowski, Dezydery. *Memoirs of a Polish Lancer. The Pamietniki of Dezydery Chlapowski,* Chicago: Emperor's Press, 1992.

Clausewitz, Carl von. *On War.* Princeton: Princeton University Press, 1976.

D'Abernon, Viscount. *The Eighteenth Decisive Battle of the World,* (London: Hodder and Stoughton), 1931.

Jomini, Henri de. *The Art of War.* London: Greenhill Books, 2006.

"Locarno Treaty," October 16, 1925, League of Nations Treaty Series 54, no. 1295, pt. 1,2 (1926): 329-39.

Pilsudski, Joseph, and Mickhail Tukhachevsky. *Year 1920 and its Climax: Battle of Warsaw during the Polish-Soviet war 1919-1920.* New York: Pilsudski Institute of America, 1972.

Treaty of Versailles. *Treaty with Poland, Treaty of Peace between the United States of America, The British Empire, France, Italy, and Japan and Poland.* Washington D.C.: Washington Government Printing Office, 1919.

SECONDARY SOURCES

Archibald Alison, *History of Europe from the Fall of Napoleon in 1815 to the Accession of Louis Napoleon in 1852.* London: William Blackwood and Sons, 1852.

Bade, Klaus. *Migration in European History.* Oxford: Blackwell Publishing, 2003.

Barber, William. *From New Era to New Deal: Herbert Hoover, the Economists, and American Economic Policy, 1921-1933.* Cambridge: Cambridge University Press, 1985.

Bishop, Chris. *Campaigns of World War II Day by Day.* London: Amber Books, 2009.

Boak, A.E.R. *The Growth of Western Civilization.* New York: Appleton Century Crofts, Inc., 1951.

Brandes, George. *Poland, A Study of the Land, People, and Literature.* New York: MacMillan Company, 1903.

Bruce, Robert, Iain Dickie, and Keven Kiley. *Fighting Techniques of the Napoleonic Age.* New York: St. Martin's Press, 2008.

Budurowycz, Bohdan. *Polish Soviet Relations 1932-1939.* New York: Columbia University Press, 1939.

Butterwick, Richard. *Poland's Last King and English Culture, Stanislaw August Poniatowski: 1732-1798.* Oxford: Oxford University Press. 1998.

Cardwell, Ann, *Poland and Russia: The Last Quarter Century,* (New York: Sheed and Ward, 1944), 12.*1732-1798.* Oxford: Clarenton Press, 1998.

Chamberlain, William. *The Russian Revolution.* United States: Macmillan Company, 1965.

Chandler, David G. *The Campaigns of Napoleon.* New York: MacMillan Publishing Company, 1966.

Citino, Robert. *Blitzkrieg to Desert Storm: the Evolution of Operational Warfare.* Lincoln: University of Kansas Press, 2004.

—. *The German Way of War: from the Thirty Year's War to the Thrid Reich.* Lincoln: University of Kansas Press, 2008.

—. *The Path to Blitzkrieg: Doctrine and Training in the German Army, 1920-1939.* Mechanicsburg: Stackpole Books, 2008.

Conquest, Robert. *The Great Terror, a Reassessment.* Oxford: Oxford University Press, 1991.

Cooper, Mathew. *The German Army.* Lanham: Scarborough House, 1978.

Cornish, Nick. *The Russian Army 1914-1918.* Oxford: Osprey, 2001.

Corum, James. *The Roots of Blitzkreig, Hans von Seeckt and German Military Reform.* (Lawrence: University of Kansas Press), 1994.

Creveld, Martin van. *The Art of War: War and Military Thought.* New York: HarperCollins Publishing, 2005.

—. *The Changing Face of War. Lessons of Combat, from the Marne to Iraq.* New York: Ballatine Books, 2006.

Davis, W.J.K. *German Army Handbook: 1939-1945.* New York: Arco Publishing, 1973.

Davies, Norman. *God's Playground, A History of Poland: The Origins to 1795.* New York: Columbia University Press, 1982.

—. *God's Playground: A History of Poland 1795 to the Present.* New York: Columbia University Press, 1982.

—. *Heart of Europe: A Short History of Poland.* Oxford: Oxford University Press, 1986

—. *No Simple Victory. World War II in Europe, 1939-1945.* New York: Penguin Group, 2006.

—. *White Eagle, Red Star.* London: Randon House E-Books, Pimlico Electronic Book Edition, 2003.

Davis, W.J.K. *German Army Handbook: 1939-1945.* New York: Arco Publishing, 1973.

Debicki, Roman. *Foreign Policy of Poland: 1919-1939.* New York: Frederick A. Praeger Publishing, 1962.

Debo, Richard. *Survival and Consolidation: The Foreign Policy of Soviet Russia, 1918-1992,* Kingston: McGill-Queen's University Press, 1992.

Doew, Dieter. *Europe in 1848, Revolution and Reform.* New York: Berghahn Books, 2001.

Dunham, Samuel Astley. *The History of Poland.* London: A & R Spottiswoode, 1858.

Evans, Richard. *The Coming of the Third Reich.* New York: Penguin Press, 2004.

Eversley, Lord. *The Partitions of Poland.* New York: Dodd, Mead, and Company, 1819.

Fisher, Todd, *The Napoleonic Wars: The Empires Fight Back, 1808-1812.* London: Osprey Publishing, 2001.

Fletcher, James.*The History of Poland from the Earliest to the Present Time* New York: Harper and Brothers, 1840.

Gat, Azar. *A History of Military Thought.* Oxford: Oxford University Press, 2001.

George, David. *Atlas of World War II.* London: Amber Books, 2008.

Gross, Jan. *Polish Society under German Occupation.* Princeton: Princeton University Press, 1979.

Halecki, Oscar. *A History of Poland.* New York: Roy, 1956.

—. *A History of Poland, New Edition.* New York: Dorset Press, 1992.

—. *Foreign Policy of Poland: 1919-1939.* New York: Praeger Publishing, 1962.

Halecki, Oscar, and W.F. Penson. *The Cambridge History of Poland: From August II to Pilsudski, 1697-1935.* Cambridge: Cambridge University Press, 1941.

Harring, Harro. *Poland under the Dominion of Russia.* Washington D.C.: Kane and Company, 1834.

Harrisson, Richard. *Architect of Soviet Victory in World War II: The Life and Theories of G.S. Isserson.* Jefferson: McFarland and Company Inc., Publishers, 2010.

Hart, B. H. Liddel. *Strategy.* London: Praeger Publishing, 1972.

Hastings, Max. *Das Reicht: The March of the 2nd SS Panzer Division though France.* New York: Holt, Rinehart, and Winston Publishing, 1981.

Havers, Robin. *Essential Histories. The Second World War, Europe 1939-1943.* Oxford: Osprey Publishing, 2002.

Heine, Marc. *Poland: How they live and work.* New York: Praeger, 1975.

Henry, Edward. *The Political History of Poland.* New York: The Polish Importing Company, 1917.

Humphrey, Grace. *Pilsudski Builder of Poland.* New York: Scott and More, 1936.

J. Johnson, Gaynor. *Lacorno Revisted, European Diplomacy, 1920-1929.* New York: Routledge, 2004.

Johnson, Lonnie. *Central Europe: Enemies, Neighbors, and Friends.* Oxford: Oxford University Press, 1996.

Keegan, John. *The Second World War.* New York: Penguin Group, 2005.

Kramer, John Horne and Alan. *German Atrocities, 1914, A History of Denial.* New Haven: Yale University Press, 2001.

Krycznski, J.N. *The Recovery of Poland.* Philadelphia: Kryczynski and Wasilewski, 1847.

Kuhn, Thomas. *The Structure of Scientific Revolutions.* Chicago: University of Chicago Press, 1996.

Lardner, Dionysius. *The History of Poland in One Volume.* London: A&R Spottiawoode, 1831.

Machray, Robert. *Poland: 1914-1931.* London: George Alled and Unwin Limited, 1932.

Macksey, Kennth. *Tank Warfare.* New York: Stein and Day Publishers, 1972.

Madej, Steve Zaloga and W. Victor. *The Polish Campaign, 1939.* New York: Hippocrene Books, 1985.

McKinley, Albert Edward. *The World War.* New York: American Book Company, 1919.

Messenger, Charles. *The Blitzkreig Story.* New York: Charles Scribner's Sons, 1976.

Mets, Harold Winton and David. *The Challenge of Change. Military Instiutions and New Realities, 1918-1941.* Lincoln: University of Nebraska Press, 2000.

Michta, Andrew. *Red Eagle: The Army in Polish Politics, 1944-1988.* Stanford: Hoover Institution, 1932.

Morfill, William Richard. *Poland.* London: T. Fisher Unwin, 1900.

—. *The Story of Poland.* New York: G.O. Putnam's Sons, 1893.

Murray, Williamson. *Strategy for Defeat: The Luftwaffe 1933-1945.* Maxwell Air Force Base: Air University Press, 2004.

Neugebauer, Mieczyskaw. *the Defence of Poland, September 1939.* Charlottesville: University of Virginia Publishing, 1942.

Norman, Louis E. Van. *Poland: The Knight Among Nations.* New York: Fleming H. Revell Company, 1908.

Overy, Richard. *1939. Countdown to War.* New York: Viking, 2009.

Paret, Peter. *Makers of Modern Strategy.* Princeton: Princeton University Press, 1986.

Parker, Geoffrey. *The Cambridge Illustrated History of Warfare.* New York: Cambridge University Press, 2009.

Peszke, Michael. *Poland's Navy, 1918-1945.* New York: Hippocrene Books, 1999.

Phillips, W. Alison. *Modern Europe: 1815-1899.* London: Rivingtons, 1902.

—. *Poland.* New York: Henry Hold and Company, 1915.

Phillips, Michael Krause and R. Cody. *Historical Perspectives of the Operational Art.* Washington D.C.: Center for Military History, 2007.

Phillips, T.R. *Roots of Strategy.* Harrisburg: Stackpole Books, 1985.

Piotr Wandycz, *France and her Eastern Allies,* (Minneapolis: University of Minnesota Press), 214.

Posen, Barry. *The Sources of Military Doctrine: France, Britain, and Germany between the World Wars.* Ithica: Cornell University Press, 1984.

Reese, Roger. *The Soviet Military Experience.* London: Routledge, 2000.

Reynolds, Paul. *A Primer in Theory Construction.* Needham Heights: Allyn and Bacon, 1971.

Richmond, Yale. *From Da to Yes: Understanding the East Europeans.* Yarmouth: Intercultural Press, 1996.

Robert Bruce, Iain Dickie, Kevin Kiley, Michael Pavkovic, Frederic Schneid. *Fighting Techniques of the Napoleonic Age: 1792-1815, Equipment, Combat Skills, and Tactics.* New York: St. Martin's Press, 2008.

Sanford, George. *Military Rule in Poland.* New York : St. Martin's Press, 1980.

Scott, Hamish M. *The Emergence of the Eastern Powers, 1756-1775.* Cambridge: Cambridge University Press, 2001.

Seidner, Stanley. *Marshal Edward Smigly-Rydz and Poland: 1935-1939.* New York: St. John's University, 1975.

Sharp, Samuel. *Poland. White Eagle on a Red Field.* Cambridge: Harvard University Press, 1953.

Stone, David. *A Military History of Russia: from Ivan the Terrible to the war in Chechnya.* Westport: Praeger, 2006.

—. *Hitler's Army: The men, machines, and organization.* Minneapolis: Zenith Press, 2009.

Snyder, Timothy. *Bloodlands: Europe Between Hitler and Stalin.* New York: Basic Books, 2010.

United States Military Academy. *The Campaign in Poland, 1939.* West Point: United States Military Academy, 1941.

Wallach, Jehuda. *The Dogma of the Battle of Annihilation.* Westport: Greenwood Press, 1986.

Wandycz, Piotr. *France and her Eastern Allies.* Minneapolis: University of Minnesota Press, 1962.

—. *The Lands of Partitioned Poland.* Seattle: University of Washington Press, 1974.

Watt, Richard M. *Bitter Glory: Poland and its Fate, 1918-1939.* New York: Hippocrene Books, 1998.

Wawro, Geoffrey. *The Franco-Prussian War. The German Conquest of France in 1870-1871.* New York: Cambridge University Press, 2003.

Williamson, David. *Poland Betrayed: the Nazi Invasions of 1939.* Mechanicsburg: Stackpole Books, 2009.

Winton, David Mets and Harold. *The Challenge of Change. Military Institutions and New Realities, 1918-1941.* Lincoln: University of Nebraska Press, 2000.

Wolski, Kalixt. *Poland: Her Glory, Her Sufferings, Her Overthrow.* London: Kerby and Endean, 1883.

Zaloga, Steven. *Poland 1939: The Birth of Blitzkrieg.* Oxford: Osprey, 2003

—. *The Polish Army 1939-1945.* Oxford: Osprey Publishing, 1982.

Zaloga, Steven and and Leland Ness. *Red Army Handbook. 1939-1945.* Thrupp: Sutton Publishing, 1998.

Zamoyski, Adam. *The Polish Way.* New York: Hippcrene Books, 2000.

—. *Warsaw 1920: Lenin's Failed Conquest of Europe.* London: Harper Collins, 2008.

Zweig, Ferdynand. *Poland between Two Wars.* London: Secker and Warburg, 1944.

INTERNET SOURCES

Bower, Bruce. *The Peace Racket.* Summer 2007. http://www.city-journal.org/html/17_3_peace_racket.html (accessed August 15, 2011).

Eternal World Television Network, *Encyclical of Pope Gregory XVI on Civil Obedience*. June 9, 1832. http://www.ewtn.com/library/ENCYC/G16CUMPR.HTM (accessed January 13, 2012).

Humanistas International. *Hitler's Speech at Danzig, Speech of September 19, 1939.* Februrary 21, 2001. http://www.humanitas-international.org/showcase/chronography/speeches/1939-09-19.html (accessed December 6, 2011).

Najder, Jacek. *Polish Cavalrymen in the French Imperial Guard.* 2012. Permanent Delegation of the Republic of Poland to North Atlantic Treaty Organization. http://www.brukselanato.polemb.net/index.php? (accessed January 12, 2012).

NASK. *The Interwar Period.* 2011. http://www.poland.pl/archives/interwar/index.htm (accessed October 4, 2011).

Navy, Polish. *1939-1947, Polish Navy Homepage.* 2009. http://www.polishnavy.pl/PMW/history/index_03.html (accessed December 2, 2011).

Niehorster, Leo. *World War II Armed Forces: Orders of Battle and Organizations.* March 20, 2005. http://niehorster.orbat.com/029_poland/organizations/_1939.html (accessed July 20, 2011).

Obee, Dave. "Volhynia." Volynian History. http://www.volhynia.com/history.html, (accessed November 12, 2011).

Krupinsky, Michael. "The Polish Army in France, World War I." Hallers Army. http://www.hallersarmy.com (accessed January 12, 2012).

Lacquement, Richard. *In the Army Now.* September 2010. http://www.the-american-interest.com/article.cfm?piece=860 (accessed September 12, 2011).

Menning, Bruce W. *Operational Art's Origins.* June 1, 2007. http://www.history.army.mil/books/OpArt/introduction.htm (accessed September 8, 2011).

Sokolowski, Henryk. *German Invasion of Poland During World War 2.* 2011. http://felsztyn.tripod.com/germaninvasion/id11.html (accessed December 2, 2011).

Soylent Communications. *Charles Francois Dumouriez.* October 24, 2011. http://www.nndb.com/people/398/000104086/ (accessed October 24, 2011).

United States Holocaust Memorial Museum. *German Prewar Expansion.* January 6, 2012. http://www.ushmm.org/wlc/en/article.php?ModuleId=10005439 (accessed January 16, 2012). (accessed January 16, 2012).

United States Library of Congress. *A Country Study: Poland.* October 1992. http://lcweb2.loc.gov/frd/cs/pltoc.html (accessed January 5, 2012).

JOURNALS, ARTICLES, AND RESEARCH PAPERS

Anderson, Joseph. "The Case for a Joint Military Decision Making Process." *Military Review*, September 2003: 11-19.

Farman, Elbert. "The Polish Bolshevik Cavalry Campains of 1920." *The Cavalry Journal*, 1921: 229-246.

Halecki, Oscar. "Imperialism in Slavic and East European History." *American Slavic and East European Review* 11, no. 1 (February 1952). http://www.jstor.org/stable/2491662 (accessed November 14, 2011).

Hodson, Fremont. *A Study on the Russo-Polish War of 1920: First Phase to include the Occupation of Kiev.* Graduate Paper, Fort Leavenworth, KS: The Command and General Staff School, 1935.

House, Johnathan. *Toward Combined Arms Warfare: A Survey of 20th Century Tactics. Doctrine, and Organization.* Fort Leavenworth, KS: Command and General Staff College, 1984.

Jonasz, Maciej. "The Poles in World War I." *Strategy and Tactics*, January 2012: 20-28.

—. "The State of the Polish Military in 1939." *World at War*, December 2010: 36-46.

Krams, Cortlandt. *A Study on the Russo-Polish War 1920: Second Phase to include the Advance of Russian Forces to the Door of Warsaw.* Graduate Research Paper, Fort Leavenworth, KS: Command and General Staff School, 1935.

Littell, E. "Polish Proverb." *The Museum of Foreign Literature, Science and Art, Volume 19*, 1831: 477.

Miranda, Joseph. "The Rhineland War: What if World War II Started in 1936?" *World at War*, December 2011: 6-16.

Schildroth, William. *A Detailed Study of the Russo-Polish War of 1920: Third Phase, the Battle of Warsaw.* Fort Leavenworth, KS: Command and General Staff School, 1935.

Smith, A O. *A Study on the Russo-Polish War 1920: Translation from the French of Chapters IV to VIII.* Graduate Research Paper, Fort Leavenworth, KS: Command and General Staff School, 1936.

Vego, Milan. "On Military Theory." *Joint Forces Quarterly*, 2011: 59-66.

Worrell, Harold. *The Battle of Warsaw, 1920: Impact on Operational Thought.* Graduate Research Paper, Fort Leavenworth, KS: School of Advanced Military Studies, 1994.

www.ingramcontent.com/pod-product-compliance
Lightning Source LLC
Chambersburg PA
CBHW081748280526
45789CB00008B/2783